The Jubilee Years

1887–1897

THE JUBILEE YEARS

1887–1897

compiled by
Roger Hudson

LONDON
The Folio Society
1996

Typeset at The Folio Society.
Printed in Great Britain by Bath Press Colourbooks
on Fineblade Cartridge paper.
Bound at The Bath Press, Avon.

Frontispiece: Queen Victoria by von Angeli

Contents

COSTUMES AT HER MAJESTY'S FANCY DRESS BALL AT BUCKINGHAM PALACE, ILLUSTRATING THE TIME OF GEORGE II., JUNE 6, 1845

HER MAJESTY THE QUEEN AS QUEEN PHILIPPA, AND THE PRINCE CONSORT AS EDWARD III., AT THE PLANTAGENET BALL AT BUCKINGHAM PALACE, MAY 12, 1842

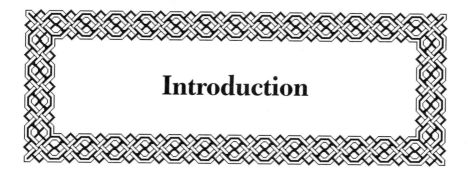

Introduction

If one were so unwise as to try to impose a pattern on history, then Great Britain's in the nineteenth century would divide, more or less neatly, into four. To appreciate fully the Jubilee decade—that culmination within the final quarter—it is necessary to look back at the rest of the century.

Until the 1830s there was still a gamey flavour about, emanating from the Prince Regent (George IV) and what E. F. Benson called Queen Victoria's other 'rather dreadful uncles . . . the days of the Brighton Pavilion and the revels of Carlton House'. Only with Victoria's marriage to Prince Albert in 1840 did respectability and sobriety start to advance, as the scene changed to Osborne and Balmoral. Over the next twenty years, with Albert's help, Victoria 'knit the monarchy, which indeed was getting very much frayed and tattered, into a most durable piece'—Benson again. Just how frayed can be seen from a report in *The Times* dated 18 January 1840:

> Her Majesty's speech delivered upon the reassembling of Parliament was, as usual, insipid and uninstructive. Its preferred topic was Her Majesty's approaching marriage, a matter of little importance or interest to the country, except as it may thereby be burdened with additional and unnecessary expense.

The threats and stresses behind the Great Reform Bill in 1832 and then the Repeal of the Corn Laws in 1846—the rick burning, riots, Luddism and Chartism which spread through country and town—gradually subsided as the 'Hungry Forties' turned into the 'Age of Equipoise', the label given to the Fifties. Britain's leading position in the world was underlined by the Great Exhibition of 1851. The earnestness of Albert and the domesticity and devotion to duty of the Queen mirrored the virtues of the middle class, which had now come into its own. Following the royal example, much of the aristocracy and gentry adopted similar colouring. The earlier wave of official reports and legislation, which sought to improve the health and working conditions of the poor,

A Golden Jubilee souvenir showing Victoria and Albert in a domestic scene, and in fancy dress at the Plantagenet Ball in 1842

subsided. Once the Crimean War was won and the Indian Mutiny quelled, peace reigned, while *laissez-faire* and retrenchment became the order of the day.

The first overt crack in the façade—the signal for the entry into the third quarter—can be dated to 1859, and the publication of Darwin's *Origin of Species*. The religious revival, which had been such a feature of life in the first half of the century, now began its retreat before a growing tide of secularism. The geologists had begun to chip away at the edifice of Faith; indeed Ruskin had complained that during every church service he could hear the dreadful tapping of their hammers. They were soon abetted by the biologists, anthropologists and practitioners of German biblical criticism. Not that there was any immediate loss of moral tone. Who can forget F. W. H. Myers's reminiscence of George Eliot, in Trinity Fellows' garden at Cambridge in 1873:

> taking as her text the three words which have been used so often as inspiring trumpet-calls of men—*God, Immortality, Duty*—[and pronouncing] with terrible earnestness, how inconceivable was the *first*, how unbelievable the *second*, and yet how peremptory and absolute the *third*.

In 1861 the Queen was devastated by the death of Prince Albert. E. F. Benson wrote:

> For many years she retired into a complete seclusion, and made no public appearances of any sort. Though for a time she would not even see her ministers, her devotion to her duty reasserted itself and she worked as hard as ever, but her labours were as secret and invisible as those of the queen-bee in the central darkness of the hive . . . During all this period the Queen remained socially cataleptic, and we can no longer refer to her as typical of what was going on.

The later 1860s saw a quickening of the legislative process once more, with the Second Reform Act of 1867 further extending the vote, the ending of the purchase of commissions in the Army, and the introduction of competitive exams for entry to the Civil Service. In 1870 compulsory elementary education was introduced and soon publishers were responding with newspapers and magazines for the newly literate. The voting power of the middle classes was being diluted at the same time as their monopoly of knowledge was eroded.

In 1866 the Prussians had defeated the Austrians at the battle of Königgrätz, so confirming themselves as the dominant German state in

8

Central Europe; their defeat of the French at Sedan in 1870, and creation of the German Empire in 1871, made them the dominant Continental power and so a new threat to Britain, replacing France, her traditional rival. This was a blow to Britain's self-confidence, and the upsurge of public enthusiasm for Imperial expansion, which can be traced to the 1870s, was in some sense a compensatory device. Disraeli, ever sensitive to the public mood, suggested in 1877 that the Queen adopt the title of Empress of India. The other Imperial stimulus was the increasing number of war correspondents, able to send their stories quickly back by telegraph to their newspapers, and so feed the public appetite for glory and adventure. The 'New Imperialism' did nothing for Britain's popularity with the Continental powers or America, all fiercely jealous of her position until well into the next century. One foreigner remarked that the sun never set on the Empire because God would not trust an Englishman in the dark.

The aristocratic and landed interests had predicted ruin for themselves when the restrictions on foreign imports were ended by the Repeal of the Corn Laws in 1846, but it did not happen—or not for nearly thirty years. When the Agricultural Depression came in 1873 it was caused by cheap grain flooding in, thanks to new railways in Europe and North America, big cuts in maritime freight costs, and refrigerated ships bringing cheap meat. A loaf which cost l*s*. 5½*d*. in 1873 was only 4½*d*. in 1905. The Duke of Marlborough might marry a Vanderbilt and the Earl of Rosebery a Rothschild, but the aristocracy never recovered from this blow to its income. The last two decades of the century belonged to the middle-class professionals, and to the new plutocrats. These were not the manufacturers and merchants of earlier years, but rather the financiers, the owners of the new stores, the men who had done well in the gold and diamond mines out in South Africa, and who now hobnobbed with the Prince of Wales and gave him good investment tips.

The final alteration, among those accumulating between the end of the Fifties and the beginning of the Eighties, was that change in taste and attitudes towards the arts known as the Aesthetic Movement. It was in part a reaction against the sobriety, dullness and philistine bad taste of the Victorian heyday, and in part a response to the fulminations of John Ruskin and William Morris about the social and psychological damage caused by the Industrial Revolution. If there were doubts creeping in about conventional religion, all the more reason for beauty to be worshipped, and art practised and enjoyed for its own sake. In 1895 Max Beerbohm poked gentle fun at the Movement in an article in the *Yellow Book* simply entitled '1880':

9

That bygone epoch when society was first inducted into the mysteries of art ... Peacock feathers and sunflowers glittered in every
room, the curio shops were ransacked for the furniture of [Queen]
Annish days, men and women, fired by the fervid works of the young
Oscar [Wilde], threw their mahogany into the streets. A few smart
women even dressed themselves in suave draperies and unheard-of
greens.

By 1880 the ingredients for the Jubilee decade were really all assembled—except for the Queen herself. But Time is a great healer and even
Victoria could not resist its ministrations: it was now twenty years since
the death of Albert. Also, as Lytton Strachey pointed out,

The nation's attitude towards her, critical and even hostile as it had
been for so many years, altogether changed ... Many causes led to
this result. Among them were the repeated strokes of personal mis-
fortune which befell the Queen during a cruelly short space of years.
In 1878 the Princess Alice, who had married in 1862 the Prince Louis
of Hesse-Darmstadt, died in tragic circumstances. In the following
year the Prince Imperial, the only son of the Empress Eugénie [of
France], to whom Victoria, since the catastrophe of 1870, had become
devotedly attached, was killed in the Zulu War. Two years later, in
1881, the Queen lost Lord Beaconsfield [Disraeli], and, in 1883, John
Brown. In 1884 the Prince Leopold, Duke of Albany, who had been
an invalid from birth, died prematurely, shortly after his marriage.
Victoria's cup of sorrows was indeed overflowing; and the public, as
it watched the widowed mother weeping for her children and her
friends, displayed a constantly increasing sympathy.

An event which occurred in 1882 revealed and accentuated the
feelings of the nation. As the Queen, at Windsor, was walking from
the train to her carriage, a youth named Roderick Maclean fired a pistol at her from a distance of a few yards. An Eton boy struck up
Maclean's arm with an umbrella before the pistol went off; no damage
was done, and the culprit was at once arrested.

Lytton Strachey went on to underline the conjunction between the
Queen's long-held instincts about Britain's conduct abroad and the new
Imperialist urges overcoming her people. The classic liberalism of
Gladstone was increasingly out of step and the final release of the Queen
from her self-imposed seclusion into the arms of her now-besotted subjects followed swiftly on Lord Salisbury's victory at the General Election
of 1886.

10

A Diamond Jubilee souvenir featuring the Charge of the Light Brigade, a naval engagement and the Battle of Tel-el-Kebir

It all sounds like some fairy story on the theme of the sleeping princess and, indeed, it is important to be reminded that real history has a way of trailing loose ends and being cluttered up with exceptions. For instance, in February 1887 Lady Monkswell, the rather timid and increasingly conservative wife of a Liberal Peer (and much quoted in the pages that follow), had to be reassured by her husband that the end of the world as she knew it was not nigh:

> On the way to church this morning I was much comforted by Bob expressing the most supreme contempt for a fear which I have meditated upon a good deal lately—it is this: That with all the appalling changes pressing upon us politically on every side, a threatened European war, Ireland upside down, the paralysis of Parliamentary government, and the exceeding badness of the Prince of Wales, it would be wise to prepare a refuge for ourselves when the deluge comes. Suppose the rates and taxes are doubled and our investments don't pay at all, what we must do is to get some little country place and farm in which we can supply ourselves with the necessities of life, because we should be cleared out of *here* in double quick time. My idea was to face boldly this state of affairs, and I am glad to say that when I unfolded my fears to Bob he was exceedingly scornful, and called me an *old Tory*.

Again, at the end of 1896, Rudyard Kipling returned to England to live in the West Country after four years in the United States. From his reaction, it is plain that there were still enclaves where the changes of the Sixties and Seventies had made precious little impact:

> I have been studying my fellow-countrymen from the outside . . . We are a rummy breed—and O Lord the ponderous wealthy society. Torquay is such a place as I do desire acutely to upset by dancing through it with nothing on but my spectacles. Villas, clipped hedges, and shaved lawns; fat old ladies with obese landaus—the Almighty is a discursive and frivolous trifler compared with some of 'em.

By then, Queen Victoria was a 'fat old lady' and the sight of a naked Kipling would undoubtedly have displeased her. But one suspects that Kipling would not have included her in his condemnation.

ROGER HUDSON

The Jubilee Years

Buying Golden Jubilee decorations

1887: The Golden Jubilee

The summer was what Queen Victoria's subjects called 'Queen's weather'. The painter Edward Burne-Jones confirmed this, tongue in cheek: 'Never was such a summer since one I remember in Lebanon before the Flood, when I attended divine worship at Astarte's Church. So I have basked and been at peace. It was all like one day, nothing happened, the sun beat upon the hills, and they were covered with wheat-sheaves, making tears gather to the eyes.' Before the Jubilee proper in June, Londoners had a diversion in the form of the American Exhibition at Earl's Court. Lord Ronald Gower, a brother of the Duke of Sutherland, recalled that its great feature was 'the famous scout, Buffalo Bill, alias the Hon. W. Cody, and his cow-boys'. Gower accompanied the Queen when she paid a visit on 21 May:

Some of us went in the Deadwood Coach, which, driven at a great rate round the arena, is attacked by mounted Indians, and much firing takes place from within and outside that vehicle. The Queen seemed delighted with the performance; she looked radiant. At the close of the performance, Buffalo Bill, at Her Majesty's desire, was presented, as well as the Indian chief, 'Red Skin', and two of the squaws with their 'papooses', whose little painted faces the Queen stroked. Her Majesty, who had driven into the exhibition in a carriage-and-four, with outriders in scarlet, left soon after six *en route* for Windsor.

As early as mid February the Viceroy of India, Lord Dufferin, wrote to the Queen's private secretary, Sir Henry Ponsonby, asking him to 'inform Her Majesty that all the ladies of Calcutta are ordering Jubilee bustles'. It is doubtful whether the message was passed on. The young Beatrix Potter and her family left the decorating of their London house until the very day before the Jubilee procession and thanksgiving service:

On Monday we were very busy arranging our fairy lights, on each of the nine front window sills, seven red in each length, five white above and three blue at the top. The Square are mostly hanging bottles and paper lanterns, the latter very pretty but most unsafe. After lunch mamma and I were greatly excited to see the Westgarths set out three flags, we having none. An anxious watch was kept on our neighbour and enemy Mr Saunders. Nothing happened during the afternoon, but at tea, a small crowd was noticed. Mr Saunders was letting down a rope with six small banners attached, from the top floor window. We hurried out in a cab and procured an immense Union Jack at a fancy price. There was not a yard of Turkey red to be had at any price. I wish we had had an idea flags would be so general. Three-quarters of the houses have them, there is only one in this Square without.

The Queen had what she called 'a large family dinner' at Buckingham Palace. Thanks to the ramifications of her children's and grandchildren's marriages, there was little false modesty in such a description, in spite of there being more than fifty Royal and Serene Highnesses present, including the Kings of Denmark, Greece and Belgium either next to or opposite her. Lady Monkswell and her husband were lucky enough to get tickets for seats inside Westminster Abbey for the great day, 21 June:

I must say that I was sick with nervousness beforehand whether I should feel up to it, whether the children would be squeezed to death in the crowd, whether the Irishmen would take that opportunity of blowing us all up together—Queen, Lords and Commons in the Abbey. I settled in my own mind I would *chance* this.

We started at nine, and drove by the river so as to avoid the line of carriages and met with no stop at all till we got to Abingdon Street quite close to the Abbey. Old Palace Yard was full of carriages and people, but we drove straight up to Peers' Entrance and got out there just as usual. We went up into Mr Bethell's [Chief Clerk in the House of Lords] room, and I amused myself with looking out of the window upon the sea of carriages, many with gorgeous fat coachmen and two footmen in splendid liveries carrying batons. It was London gone mad, I could hardly believe that the balconies and stands, windows and roofs were covered with reasonable mortals like myself. The Royal Standard was flying in fine style from the top of St Margaret's. I detected the bulky figure of Lord Salisbury [the Prime Minister] in a Privy Councillor's uniform, walking across from the Abbey. About ten o'clock I thought we would go and see the fun so I got up and went into the House of Lords library and all about the place. It was just like a party, all the peers in uniform, and the ladies very smart.

I sat on the Woolsack for a time, and wondered where I should get to next. We were told that the Chancellor followed by the peers would go

across to the Abbey at a quarter to eleven, but at half-past ten I thought
we had better be on the scene of action so we went out, and a friendly
policeman told us the procession of Chancellor etc. had just started, so
we ran as hard as we could down a passage and joined them just at Westminster Hall. We proceeded across the road in a most impressive manner, I daresay there were 500 or 600 peers and peeresses, and walked
into the Abbey at Poets' Corner. In our south transept were built up
three galleries; we were far back on the lowest. The one over our heads
came down so far that I could only see our corresponding gallery in the
north transept and not a bit of the chancel or of the nave. The walls
seemed completely covered with wooden shields, so that not a monument was to be seen and only an occasional glimpse of a painted window.
We climbed into our places rather unceremoniously, several kind peers
giving me a hand over the benches. Our nineteen inches of seat was not
really so very uncomfortable, though there were no backs. Just exactly in
front of me sat Lady Burdett-Coutts [the famous philanthropist] in a
splendid gown covered with silver braid and pearls: she was most kind
to me and implored me whenever we stood up—as we did on the slightest provocation, we got so bored with waiting—to hold on to her shoulder. She wore a broad red ribbon, some order or other, across her right

A State Banquet at
Buckingham Palace

shoulder. Next to her was a very old and funny Lord Crewe, who was not at all satisfied with his seat and groaned and climbed about *on his knees* across the benches. He was so extremely aged that I feel sure the effort would have killed him if Lady B-C had not held his stick, while Bob caught hold of his cocked hat and very high feather.

When we had been seated about three-quarters of an hour some Oriental princess and the Queen of Hawaii were escorted in by the chamberlains and took their seats in the chancel. But we began to get dreadfully tired of it, and were almost bursting with impatience when we heard a flourish of trumpets which meant that the Queen had arrived. We did not know whether she might not be going to take off her bonnet and put on her crown. We were all standing up, I on the extreme of my toes and on the seat, when, escorted by the Lord Chamberlain, she came in. It was too far off to see the expression of her face, but I could see that she was flushed, but not the least flurried. She bowed twice, I think to our side, and took her seat on the throne. Then all the princes and princesses (there were thirty or thirty-five of them) filed round in front of her, bowed, and passed on to take their seats. She was dressed in black with the blue ribbon of the Garter over her shoulder, she had a white lace bonnet and strings, and I could see jewels sparkling round the front when she moved her head. The service itself lasted about forty minutes. The *Te Deum* set to music by Prince Albert, an anthem and some prayers. Although there was an immense choir and trumpets and violoncellos, the Abbey was so packed with people that at times I could only *just* hear them. About forty or fifty of the peers and peeresses behaved very badly in scuttling out when it was half over so as to get a view of the procession, and they were rewarded by missing what probably was the most interesting part of the whole concern. The Queen stood up bravely for a good part of the *Te Deum*, and joined in all the service. When it was over the Prince of Wales kissed her hand and she kissed him on the cheek. Then, one by one, all the princesses came forward, curtseyed and kissed her hand, and she kissed them on the cheek: she did it in such an interesting personal manner: one could almost see what she felt for each. She gave the Princess Royal a particularly loving kiss, in fact I think she gave her two kisses, both before and after she had kissed her hand. I wished then I could have seen their faces. When all the ladies had passed on the princes each came up and kissed her hand, and she kissed them too—at least I am not quite sure, they may have kissed her. Anyhow a greeting passed between them. Then she turned and walked down the aisle, and disappeared from view—and the great show was over.

We behaved very well as without any scurrying or shoving we walked

quietly out. When we reached the pavement, instead of going at once to the House of Lords we turned to the left and walked round by St Margaret's to see what we could of the procession, and were most fortunate as the carriages had not yet started. We saw them pass, and I got a general impression of princes on horseback and princesses in carriages, but as I had a trooper's horse looking over each of my shoulders, and when the trumpets blew the horses began to jump, it was anything but a quiet corner. We walked back across the road to the House of Lords, and began to discover that we were dying of hunger and thirst. The dining-room and passages were full of peers laden with glasses, knives and forks, and peeresses carrying off in triumph armfuls of plates. Bob and I escaped with these treasures to Mr Bethell's room, where we had a picnic lunch with Violet Bethell, and felt that we had got through this dreaded Jubilee Day most capitally. We got home about three.

As a Jubilee only comes once in a while I thought it would be interesting to ride round the Park, and see the preparations for the school-treat of 30,000 children for the next day. The Park seemed full of the inhabitants of Oxford Street and Tottenham Court Road. There were at least forty or fifty huge tents set up between the Serpentine and Marble Arch. I should not have known my own Hyde Park.

Augustus Hare, the prolific compiler of English guide books, writer of

The Royal procession passing Trafalgar Square on the way to Westminster Abbey on Jubilee Day 1887

foreign travel books and diarist, witnessed the school-treat in Hyde Park, and then the torchlight display put on by the boys of Eton College at Windsor.

A dense mass of people walled in the vast enclosed space, but all in the utmost good-humour, though many came forward with—'Oh, do give me your ticket: oh, do now, just for once.' Inside the outer barrier was a second, within which people walked, and whence they saw. I was indignant at first at not being admitted further, but when I saw the Archbishop of Canterbury refused, was quite contented to share the fate of the first subject in the realm. However, eventually we were both passed into the immense space where the children were playing, not apparently the least overdone by the hot sun, or tired from having been on the move since ten a.m., and having been provided, on arriving, with nothing but a bag containing a meat-pie, a bun, and an orange, with instructions to put the bag in their pockets when done with! Each of the 30,000 children also had a 'Jubilee mug' of Doulton ware. Every now and then volleys of tiny coloured balloons were sent up, like flights of bright birds floating away into the soft blue, and, as the royalties arrived, a great yellow balloon, with several people in its car, bore a huge 'Victoria' skywards.

Between half-past four and five Life Guards heralded a long procession of carriages, with the Indian princes, the foreign queens and kings, and our own royal family in force. A number of Eastern chieftains were riding six abreast, and very like Bluebeard one or two of them looked. Finally came the Queen, smiling, good and gracious beyond words, and with a wonderful reception everywhere.

Having escorted Lady Normanton to the safe solitudes of Wilton Place, I rushed off to Windsor, arriving at nine. I stayed on the bridge to see the thousand Eton boys cross, marching in detachments, with white and blue uniforms alternately, carrying their (then unlighted) torches,

and then went after them to the Castle, where I was one of the few admitted, and pushed on at once to the inner court under the Queen's apartments.

Most unspeakably weird, picturesque, inspiring, beautiful, and glorious was the sight, when, with a burst of drums and trumpets, the wonderful procession emerged under the old gate of Edward III, headed by a detachment of the Blues, then the boys, six abreast, carrying lighted torches, till hundreds upon hundreds had filed in, singing splendidly 'God save the Queen'. All the bigger boys formed into figures of blazing light in the great court, weaving designs of light in their march—'Welcome', 'Victoria', etc., in radiant blaze of moving living illumination; whilst the little boys, each carrying a coloured Chinese lantern on a wand, ascended in winding chains of light the staircases on the steep hill of the Round Tower opposite the Queen's window, till the slope was covered with brilliancy and colour. The little boys sang very sweetly in the still night their song of welcome, and then all the mass of the boys below, raising their flaming torches high into the air, shouted with their whole hearts and lungs, 'Rule Britannia!'

It was an unspeakably transporting scene, and I am sure that the beloved figure in the white cap seated in the wide-open central window felt it so, and was most deeply moved by the sight and sound of so much

Torchlight display by Eton boys at Windsor Castle for the Golden Jubilee

21

loyal and youthful chivalry. Then, in a great hush, she almost astonished them by leaving her place and suddenly reappearing in the open air in the courtyard amongst them, and making them a queenly and tender little speech in her clear beautiful voice—'I do thank you so very very much,' etc. And then, in figures of light from their torches, as she reappeared at the window, the vast assembly formed the word 'Good-night'.

On 25 June the distinguished scientist Sir Lyon Playfair wrote to Sir Henry Ponsonby:

On coming back from the Abbey, impressed deeply with the ceremony, I tried to form an index of the progress of civilisation during the Queen's reign. The result may interest you. The price of rags as indicating the demand for paper has always appeared to me the best index of progress and the following facts are striking:

In 1837 each head of the population consumed 1¼ lb. of paper: in 1887 no less than 12 lbs. Measured by this index England is now at the head of all nations in 1887.

England	12 lbs.,	of paper per head	
United States	10 "	"	"
Germany	9 "	"	"
France	8 "	"	"
Italy	4 "	"	"

In 1837 each person of the population spent 1*s.* 11*d.* on books and newspapers annually: in 1887 this had increased to 9*s.*

In 1837 each person sent nine letters through the post: in 1887 this had increased to thirty-eight. An index of this kind is encouraging.

Another index of well doing is the consumption of soap, because 'Cleanliness is next to Godliness'. This however has not increased so much as I could have wished:

1837–7¾ lbs. per head of soap
1887–10 lbs.   "   "

Still a child born today has three years more of life than if born in 1837.

The Governing of the Country

What qualities did the Queen bring to her part in this? What were her relations with her ministers, in their joint endeavours, not merely to increase the consumption of paper and soap, but to steer Britain and her Empire safely towards the new century? First, we hear E. F. Benson on her character. These days, Benson is best remembered for the six novels he wrote in the 1920s and 30s featuring Mapp and Lucia, which were successfully adapted for television. But in his younger days, as the entertaining son of the Archbishop of Canterbury, he was able to move effortlessly through the higher reaches of late Victorian and Edwardian Society. His memories of this vanished world, distilled in his book As We Were, *allow him to speak with perception and authority on the Queen.*

As Sovereign the Queen was a slave to her duties, and no one ever worked harder or more conscientiously at her job. This admirable devotion never left her, and up to the last years of her life, when she suffered much from such fatiguing disabilities as rheumatic joints and failing eyesight, she used often to sit up till one or two o'clock in the morning, even when on holiday, to get her work finished. She cared nothing for state and splendour in themselves, and though in the performance of her royal functions she was of a superb and wholly native dignity, thus showing that she was indeed Queen of England and knew it, it was the sense of duty that inspired her, and when her duty was done, she wanted only to get back to the freedom of privacy. [But] she could no more have lived without her Queenship and remained alive in the very vivid sense in which she was alive, than she could have lived without her lungs: being Queen was part of the air she breathed. Both as Queen and as housewife she conducted her life on broad simple principles, hating anything flamboyant or 'extraordinary', quite uninterested in problems of human nature and in the dim mysterious yearnings which inspire art and music, simple and sincere in her religion, troubled neither by ecstasy nor by theological complexities.

Queen Victoria was a woman of peerless common sense; her common sense, which is a rare gift at any time, amounted to genius. She had been brought up by her mother with the utmost simplicity, and she retained it to the end, and conducted her public and private life alike by that infallible guide. She had no imagination, no flight of fancy ever bore her away, she looked very steadily with her rather prominent blue eyes on every situation that presented itself, and made up her mind as to what was the level-headed and the sensible thing to do. But she had a sort of dual personality, which often supplies the key to the odd complexities and complications that she sometimes exhibited. One entity in her was that of Her Majesty the Queen of England, supreme (and determined to exercise her supremacy and to demand the due recognition of it) in all questions that concerned the welfare of her realm; the other entity was that of a very shrewd *bourgeoise*, and neither of these strains had much in common with aristocratic instincts and ideas. No human being of whom we have record, with the possible exception of Shakespeare, has possessed both imagination and common sense equally developed in a very high degree, for imagination gets dulled by common sense, and the bright mirror is clouded, while common sense gets dazzled by imagination. There was no such disturbing glitter in the Queen's mind: common sense poured out from her, grey and strong, like the waters of the Amazon.

Her intense admirer, Lord Beaconsfield, himself highly imaginative, once said that if he wanted to forecast the effect of some Parliamentary measure on the minds of the middle class, and distrusted his own judgement, he always consulted the Queen and always found he had been right in accepting her opinion. But it was not because she had imagination that she could foretell with such faultless precision what the middle class would feel. She was identical (in this piece of her personality) with the governing class of her subjects, which she saw, long before any of her ministers perceived it, was no longer the aristocracy who then were the landlords of the greater part of English soil, but the middle class. She had that strain in herself: she needed no imagination in order to picture what they would feel, because she knew. Thus Lord Beaconsfield's dictum, which has been so often and so erroneously taken to mean that she was a woman of commonplace mind, had no such intention, but was in reality an expression of his highest admiration for her judgement. Her mind was not in the least commonplace, it was that of a genius of common sense who knew, as a Queen who was really a Queen should know, the mentality, political and social, of that class which would shortly be supreme in her realm.

Side by side in her mind with this invaluable instinct there functioned, with no less natural vigour, her sense of Queenship. She stood

The Mother of Parliaments, moonlit, by Louis H. Grimshaw

for monarchy incarnate, just as she stood for the middle class, and all that protected and championed that sacred principle was to her sacred. Church and State were the buttresses that supported the throne, and the throne must support them, for otherwise they would all come clattering down together, and so, though officially she was of no political party, she was actually a Tory of the Tories. All legislation that threatened the solidity of these buttresses was intensely repugnant to her, and thus, though rigidly neutral officially with regard to the will of the people, she once told my father how exceedingly pleased she was, personally and privately, to think that the House of Lords would never pass Mr Gladstone's Bill for the disestablishment of the Welsh Church, and that there was no constitutional means of removing their veto. Anything, however small, that threatened to diminish the property and privileges of these buttresses must be sternly resisted.

If the Queen epitomised force of character in one direction, then so too did Gladstone in another. Disraeli said that Gladstone had not a single redeeming defect and perhaps this had something to do with the collisions between him and the Queen which were a regular feature in affairs of state from the 1870s to the 1890s. Her resistance to his attempts to disestablish the Church is touched on above; she deplored his administration's handling of events in the Sudan, that culminated in the death of General

25

Gordon in 1885. But most of all she resented his attempts to give Home Rule to the Irish, first in 1886 and then again in 1893. When she realised in the middle of 1892 that it was inevitable that he should again be Prime Minister, she did not mince her words to Sir Henry Ponsonby, calling Gladstone 'a deluded excited man of eighty-two' and saying that she did not want 'that dangerous old fanatic thrust down her throat'. She went on, 'Mr G. will find the Queen very determined and firm on all *that concerns* the *honour, dignity and* safety *of the* Vast Empire *confided to her care and which she wishes to hand down unimpaired to her children and their children's children.' E. F. Benson again:*

All that Mr Gladstone did was charged with a terrific voltage. I went more than once to Hawarden [Gladstone's house in North Wales] when, after taking my degree at Cambridge, I was archaeologically employed in examining the north wall of the City of Chester, into which had been built a quantity of tombstones from a Roman cemetery. There I had the good fortune to discover some inscribed monuments to men who had served in the Tenth Legion, 'Valeria Victrix', of which no record in Britain had hitherto come to light, and I took over to Hawarden, to show to Mr Gladstone, blotting-paper 'squeezes' of some of them. (The method of making these squeezes is to spread a sheet of damp blotting-paper over the inscription of which you desire a facsimile and then to tap it gently with a clothes-brush, until the blotting-paper has moulded itself into the lettering: when dry, it thus becomes a portable cast of the stone.) Mr Gladstone was enormously interested in the discovery of this legion having been in England, though it was only the minutest contribution to the details of the Roman occupation seventeen hundred years ago, and he got down some books of military inscriptions for reference. But equally fiery was his advice about making squeezes. The blotting-paper, he said, ought certainly to be laid down dry on the face of the inscription, and then be sprinkled: otherwise it was liable to tear. For the same reason it should be left on the stone till it was dry again: otherwise damp fragments might stick to it, and the squeeze be spoilt. I felt that Mr Gladstone had devoted his whole life to making squeezes and that he occupied his leisure only in conducting the affairs of the nation. Though Mrs Gladstone had come to remind him that lunch was ready, he would not go till he had conjectured about a few missing letters in one of these inscriptions: the thing might have been a dispatch from Downing Street which must be deciphered and dealt with at once: otherwise some hideous European imbroglio would follow. And there was the table at which his political work was done, and close by the 'Homer-table' where he found coolness and refreshment when hot with polemics.

26

Gladstone, wearing his famous collar and pince-nez

At lunch there was a discussion about the dismal task of packing a bag, when one was leaving by an early train in the morning; the sponge was wet from the traveller's ablutions and it always oozed dampness into neighbouring linen. Then came the oracle: 'You none of you know how to pack your sponge. The only way of packing a sponge is first to wrap it up in your bath towel, and then to stamp upon it.' Surely he had never done anything all his life but pack sponges in bags for early morning travel!

Everything that he was engaged in for the moment was of supreme importance: it was the same with his backgammon, with which he relaxed himself in the evening. But relaxed? He rattled and threw the dice, as if he was playing with the devil for his own immortal soul, and was temporarily engaged in a war with the powers of darkness. One afternoon he drove me to St Deiniol's, the library of his own books which he was arranging with the purpose of bequeathing them to the clergy of the Church of Wales, which he hoped to disestablish. That was exceedingly like him: his conscience told him that the Church should be disendowed, and in anticipation of that he began to endow it personally with a magnificent library, for the clergy must have access to sources of learning. A pony-carriage came round, and I was aware that he was going to drive himself. Before getting in he went round to the pony's head and peered at him. 'He's a beast,' he said, 'I must get a heavier whip.' Out he came again with this more formidable weapon, and off we went, he the intrepid charioteer of something over eighty years.

Always there was this huge concentration of force; purpose at white heat roared like a furnace in every action of his life. When once he had convinced himself on any subject, it ceased to be his opinion, and became a cosmic truth, which it was the duty of every right-minded person to uphold. Just as the only method of packing up a damp sponge was to begin by stamping on it (he being merely the exponent of this dazzling truth to an ignorant world), so he was convinced, and said so, that the will of the English people was set on giving Home Rule to Ireland, and that he was the appointed instrument to accomplish their will for them: God gave him his health and vitality for that. Thus his conscience was invariably clear of personal ambition: he was working not for his own idea but for some great cause external to him. Never, so Mrs Gladstone told my mother, did the estrangements and execrations of those who had been his friends cause him to say 'I wish I had never done it!' He might regret the bitterness he had aroused, but he never regretted those measures which had caused it.

This remorseless inflexibility was one of the reasons why in his official relation with the Queen he so often irritated her. He always paid her the most profound respect, but his deference to her person did not include the slightest deference to her statecraft and nothing she said influenced him in the least when his mind was made up, for he knew he was right, whereas she, on those many occasions when their views differed, was equally certain that he was wrong. It was therefore with the most unfeigned pleasure that she saw the fall of his last ministry in 1894, and she commented on it privately to my father with remarkable frankness: this was perfectly correct on her part for he officially had no politics any more than she. 'Mr Gladstone has gone out, disappeared all in a moment,' she gleefully observed, 'his last two ministries have been failures, indeed his last three. Mr Gladstone takes up one or two things, and then nothing else interests him. He cares nothing for foreign affairs which are always essential to England, knows nothing of foreign affairs, and is exceedingly distrusted on the Continent. They have thought he might abandon Egypt at any moment. He will not attend to any suggestion but his own

mind's. He does not care what you say, does not attend. I have told him two or three facts of which he was quite ignorant of foreign tone and temper. It makes no difference. He only says "Is that so? Really!" ' Indeed it must have been most irritating, for the Queen had an unfailing fund of first-rate common sense, and her very long experience of foreign affairs made her a far more dispassionate observer than Gladstone on the war-path for an idea. Besides, she happened to be Queen of England, and it was surely reasonable that she should expect to be listened to.

There was another reason why she disliked him, and when that was made known to him his reception of it was characteristic of the real greatness of the man and his uprightness. There had been from time to time odious and unfounded gossip of the falsest sort, arising from his interest in the deplorable women on the streets. He used to talk to them when he walked back at night, as he so often did, from the House, trying to persuade them to go home. He even brought one, with Mrs Gladstone's full knowledge and approval, into his house for a night's shelter. Very possibly he behaved imprudently, but such imprudence was due to his own consciousness of his high motive, and no one who knew him could fail to be aware of his absolute moral rectitude. The gossip had somehow

Gladstone travelling by public omnibus, by Alfred Morgan. Gladstone was a great advocate of public transport – in the 1840s he had been responsible for forcing the railway companies to run cheap third-class trains for workmen, and he had made a point of using them too

29

reached the Queen's ears, and she hinted at what she had heard to Lord Beaconsfield, who, at the least, did not tell her that there could be no truth in it, but, for whatever reason, let her continue to suspect ugly things of him. Mr Gladstone was speaking one day about the Queen's coldness and unfriendliness towards him to the late Lord Stanmore, who was an old and valued friend of his, and Lord Stanmore thought he had better tell him that the Queen suspected him of immoral behaviour with common women. Mr Gladstone's answer was one that could only have been made by a man of truly great nature. 'If the Queen thinks that of me,' he said, 'she is quite right to treat me as she does.'

G. W. E. Russell bears out the difficulties of the relationship between the Queen and her Prime Minister:

Mr Gladstone has manners but no small talk. He is so consumed by zeal for great subjects that he leaves out of account the possibility that they may not interest other people. He pays to everyone, and not least to ladies, the compliment of assuming that they are on his own intellectual level, engrossed in the subjects which engross him, and furnished with at least as much information as will enable them to follow and to understand him. Hence the genesis of that absurd story about his demeanour to the Queen.

'He speaks to Me as if I was a public meeting,' is a complaint which is said to have proceeded from illustrious lips. That most successful of all courtiers, the astute Lord Beaconsfield, used to engage Her Majesty in conversation about water-colour drawing and the third-cousinships of German princes. Mr Gladstone harangues her about the polity of the Hittites, or the harmony between the Athanasian Creed and Homer. The Queen, perplexed and uncomfortable, tries to make a digression— addresses a remark to a daughter, or proffers biscuits to a begging terrier. Mr Gladstone restrains himself with an effort till the princess has answered or the dog has sat down, and then promptly resumes: 'I was about to say —' Meanwhile the flood has gathered force by delay, and when it bursts forth again it carries all before it.

In the following extracts Lady Monkswell describes Gladstone at a dinner party in 1891, then Betty Ponsonby, daughter of the Queen's secretary Sir Henry Ponsonby, tells of the G. O. M. (Grand Old Man) at another rather more fraught dinner at Osborne in 1892. In 1893 Lord Esher stays at Windsor Castle at the same time as the Gladstones and then a future Liberal Prime Minister, Sir Henry Campbell-Bannerman, puts the Queen in her place at Balmoral.

Lady Monkswell

I was rather cross at having to go all the way to Portland Place, such a cold bad night with every prospect of a fog. I was not much more pleased on arriving at the Bryce's to be ushered into a drawing-room as cold as charity and lighted by some eight or ten electric lights so that it was considerably lighter than daylight and most unbecoming (though for that matter I was no worse off than the other women).

The door opened and in marched Mr and Mrs G. The old boy was looking quite fresh and gay, and as to Mrs Gladstone I cannot believe that she is seventy-seven or seventy-eight, she is still so handsome. In a few minutes we went down to dinner. I was rather overcome to find that I was sitting next to the G. O. M. himself. However, I knew that all that was required of me was to act the part of a devoted listener. He talked almost without intermission, ate a very good dinner, and took his share of champagne. He began first about Carlyle, and said that he was a poet who wrote in prose: he seemed to think highly of his genius but did not admire him much. Then he turned to me and I got him on the subject of Italy. He said he went there first 'fifty-nine years ago' in 1832, when he was twenty-three. It was impossible, he said, for him to describe his joy at hearing the beautiful language spoken, and he became quite enthusiastic and gesticulated with his funny old withered hands, and stretched his right arm up to heaven and said that it passed his comprehension how people could be such dolts and fools as not to learn Italian. (I

Dinner at Haddo House, *by Alfred Emslie. The Host is Lord Aberdeen – the G. O. M. is on Lady Aberdeen's right, Lord Rosebery on her left.*

31

The Lobby of the House of Commons, *by the caricaturist 'Lib'. Gladstone, next to the bespectacled Joseph Chamberlain, has Lord Randolph Churchill behind him talking to the bearded Lord Hartington (the future Duke of Devonshire), while Harry Chaplin is below the clock*

resolved to have some more lessons at once.) The best expression of his face was when he half smiled and shut up to narrow slits his fiery gleaming old eyes. He talked about Dr Schliemann (who dug out Troy); and gave us in a few eloquent words a short resumé of his life. It was beautifully told and I listened with all my ears. He looks a very old man, he is getting to look so small and shrunk, he has only some half dozen hairs *hung* round his head, and his teeth seem very much gone. But his voice is clear and ringing and, as he said, 'for the last thirty years I have felt in me the desire and determination to fight with old age'. A very successful fight so far. He said that his father ought to have lived to be a hundred. He died quite by accident of a cold, or some trifle, at eighty-seven.

The effort of listening at such a very acute angle and for so long was so great that I actually strained my left eye, which feels very queer this morning, in my desire to see as much of him as possible. I also got *no* dinner; this was no great loss as it was the worst dinner I ever saw. But when I got home I was raging hungry. I behaved very badly to Lord Thring; though he is a great friend of mine I did not talk to him at all. He very good-naturedly said, 'Never mind me, you listen to him.'

Betty Ponsonby

It was on 15 August 1892—a year after I married. I was staying alone at

Osborne Cottage, and as my mother wasn't well, I went with my father to dinner with the Queen at Osborne House, wearing my white satin wedding gown.

It proved to be a most interesting, almost historical occasion. It was the day Mr Gladstone had returned to office as Prime Minister, resolved to bring in his Home Rule Bill. We all waited in the drawing-room till, at half-past eight, she swept in. He was most obviously nervous, fumbling over his stick. Not so, the Queen. She hated having to receive him again as the Premier, but with the utmost *savoir faire* and *grâce d'état* she walked in, shook hands, and added with a smile: 'You and I, Mr Gladstone, are lamer than we used to be!' Then we all followed her into the dining-room. The Prince and Princess of Wales were also present that night, and other royalties.

I sat next to Mr Gladstone and he talked to me loudly and eagerly all the time, though guests usually spoke in hushed tones at the Queen's table. He went on openly to a glorification of the policy he advocated for Ireland. I looked at the lovely Belfast linen tablecloth, in which were woven the Rose, Thistle and Shamrock, with the motto *Quis separabit*? [who will part us?] just in front of us.

I quite forget who our other two dinner-neighbours were, but they had not much chance of conversation that night. After dinner, the Queen came straight up to me and asked: 'What did Mr Gladstone talk to you about?' 'Home Rule, ma'am!' She shrugged her shoulders and said: 'I know! . . . he always will!'

Lord Esher

I went up to London. Returned in the train with Mr and Mrs G. bound for the Castle. *He* was wonderfully alert. Nevertheless he complains that he cannot do a good day's work. 'Only five hours today,' he says; 'I am unfit for my place; drawing my pay on false pretences.' He did not sleep a wink the night before his speech [introducing the second Home Rule Bill], but he came down looking so fresh that none suspected it. His table was clear of letters. They had all been suppressed by his staff. He was furious. 'There must be letters. I must have them at once.' So a selection was found for him, and work had to be supplied all day. He had by that time his speech in his head, and had no occasion to think about it. That night (after his speech) he slept nine hours like a child. When told that a great crowd was collected in Downing Street he said, 'All to see a wretched old man of eighty-four who is past his work.'

He *walked* up to the Castle today. Mrs G. drove alone in the royal carriage sent to meet him.

The tower of St Margaret's Westminster with the north transept of the Abbey behind, by Louis H. Grimshaw

From the diaries of Charles Hobhouse, a Liberal MP.

Campbell-Bannerman was in attendance at Balmoral, and the Queen, who had been very rude over the Home Rule Bill, said at dinner one day, 'Mr Campbell-Bannerman, I don't like the way Mr Farquharson of Invercauld treats his tenants. I speak as a neighbour and not as the Queen. He is not a resident here now and his agent rackrents the tenants and will make no improvements.' When she had done, C.-B. bent forward and said, 'Well ma'am, you've admirably described a state of affairs whose existence in Ireland had made me a Home Ruler.'

When Gladstone finally resigned in 1894, Irish Home Rule was as far away as ever. An MP for more than sixty-two years, he had been Chancellor of the Exchequer for fourteen budgets, as well as the only man to serve as Prime Minister four times. He likened his relationship with the Queen over the previous five decades to that which he had with a mule when on tour in Sicily in 1838: 'I had been on the back of the beast for many scores of hours, it had done me no wrong; it had rendered me much valuable service, but it was in vain to argue; there was the fact staring me in the face. I could not get the smallest shred of feeling for the brute, I could neither love

*it nor like it. What that Sicilian mule was to me, I have been to the Queen;
and the fortnight or three weeks are represented by fifty-two or fifty-three
years.'*

E. F. Benson called Gladstone 'a cosmic and overwhelming personage',
but insisted that his opposite number among the ranks of the Tories, Lord
Salisbury, 'also belonged to the larger breed'. Larger in frame as well as
spirit: by the 1890s his size was such that no horse could carry him and so
he could be seen 'labouring on his tricycle through St James's Park in the
early hours of the day' in order to take exercise. He has been called 'a true
Tory—a practitioner of the politics of depression', but profound though
his conservatism was in most areas of life, his house at Hatfield was one of
the first to be lit by electricity. Never mind that he and his sons frequently
had to bombard the wires with cushions to put out the flames when they
shorted. An early telephone was also installed there and Lord Salisbury
was discovered testing it by reciting nursery rhymes down it.

In her biography of her father, Gwendolen Cecil recalled his failure to
recognise W. H. Smith when sitting one away from him at dinner, even
though Smith was at the time second man in Salisbury's ministry: 'The
only plea which he could urge in excuse of this wonderful blunder was that
he always sat opposite Mr Smith in Cabinet and had therefore never
learnt what his profile looked like.'

He refused to attach importance to his title: 'He would maintain that
rank without the power of which it was originally the symbol was a sham,
and the assumption, therefore, that he could be gratified by its possession
an insult to his intelligence.' In a similar vein, 'he was not aware of enjoying any pleasure whose indulgence depended on wealth.' Indeed, his two
favourite relaxations were carrying out scientific experiments and collect-
ing second-hand books on the French Revolution. He was totally without
visual taste, but luckily knew it. His own rooms at Hatfield were 'saved
from aggressive ugliness by their lack of pretension towards any standard
of appearance whatsoever—a world where the existence of outward form
was unrecognised'.

Salisbury's party lost to Gladstone and the Liberals in 1880, but
between 1886 and 1892 he was Prime Minister, until Gladstone came back
for his last Home Rule attempt. However, their rivalry was for public consumption and, according to Lady Warwick, things were quite different in
private. Frances (Daisy) Brooke, Countess of Warwick, was one of the
wealthiest as well as one of the most beautiful woman of her age. The
inspiration for the music-hall song 'Daisy, Daisy', for some years she was
the Prince of Wales's mistress. He was said to have given her an ankle
bracelet inscribed 'Heaven's Above'. In later years she was financially
embarassed and tried to sell his letters to King George V. She was bought

Lord Salisbury

off by the founder of the Dunlop Rubber Company, who was rewarded with a baronetcy. She also took up socialism, which makes her a particularly interesting witness both of her class and of politicians, as here:

Lady Salisbury asked me on one occasion to an intimate tea-party in Arlington Street, where the only other guests were Mr and Mrs Gladstone and Mr John Murray, grandson of the founder of the great publishing firm. Lord Salisbury, who was also present, sat apart with a grey Shetland shawl wound round his bearded face and shaggy head, the picture of silent misery. He had a bad toothache, it seemed. Mr Gladstone asked anxiously what he was doing about it. 'Nothing,' said Lord Salisbury. 'Nothing: hope it will pass.'

'But surely', enquired Mr Gladstone, 'you've tried Bunter's Nervine?' No, Lord Salisbury had never even heard of it. Mr Gladstone at once proposed to run out and get some, and in spite of our attempts to stop him and send a servant, he bolted from the room and speedily returned in triumph with a bottle of the Nervine. Nor would he stop there. He insisted on applying the cure for himself. He made Lord Salisbury sit back in his chair and open his mouth. I watched Mr Gladstone peer into the open jaw of his great political adversary. The offending tooth was located, Mr Gladstone carefully applied cotton wool soaked in Nervine to the tender place. In five minutes Lord Salisbury had to own that the pain was gone, and he then, to my inexpressible relief, unwound the grey shawl from his enormous head.

E. F. Benson admired Lord Salisbury's grand style: 'something Eliza-bethan, and he wore his office with the same indifference as his Garter robes, and that very indifference, the naturalness of it, was impressive'. If he had been a guest at Hatfield in July 1892 at the time of the general election, he would have seen, as did the seventeen-year-old Lady Emily Lytton, that the indifference was something of a façade. She was there with her two elder sisters, Betty and Conny, and their recently widowed mother. Their father, the Earl of Lytton, had been Viceroy of India and then Ambassador in Paris. In 1897 Lady Emily was to marry Edwin Lutyens, the architect; here she is writing to an elderly clergyman who served as a father figure:

We arrived about teatime, and as there was only Lady Salisbury and Miss Alderson [her sister] present I did not feel shy. The worst part of the day is the evening, but I lived through it and was almost happy. Poor mother is fearfully nervous and upset and I thought she would faint before dinner. Although dreadfully trying I think it is good for her. Betty and Conny both pretended to be very shy, so I felt happier. Mother gave me a lecture before dinner about talking. I can assure you I should be agreeable enough to please you or anybody if advice could make me so. Mother makes me so dreadfully shy, for she keeps calling attention to the fact that I am just out, and that this is my first visit, which she has said every time I have been anywhere for the last year. However, it has been said to Betty and Con in their turn, and I must put up with it in mine.

At dinner last night I sat between Eustace Balfour [a brother of Arthur Balfour] and one of the curates who is half a Spaniard. For some time after dinner I sat and talked to Betty, who lectured me severely on my behaviour to the curate. I told her he ought to have begun the conversation as I did not. He ought to have had pity on me, as he was not shy and I was. The chief topic was of course the elections. Everyone trying to seem indifferent to our losses, and delighted at the idea of Gladstone getting in, but they all failed hopelessly and everyone was as gloomy as possible.

Today has been one of the most exciting and sickening days I have ever spent. All the morning I passed in the garden with the children eating fruit. The excitement began just before lunch. There were five Americans coming to lunch, and we were all ordered to remain calm and indifferent before them should we hear of Jim Cranborne's* defeat.

* The Salisburys' eldest son, who had the courtesy title of Lord Cranborne.

*A garden party at Hatfield House in 1889 for the Shah of Persia. He stands in
the centre with the Princess of Wales on his left, while the Prince leans against
the balustrade with Lord and Lady Salisbury behind him. Augustus Hare, who
was present, said the Shah was 'a true Eastern potentate in his consideration for
himself and himself only . . . he wipes his wet hands on the coat-tails of the
gentleman next to him without compunction. He expressed his wonder that
Lord Salisbury did not take a new wife'*

About half an hour before lunch the telegrams began to arrive. Every
time the door opened there was nearly a scream from excitement.
Telegram after telegram arrived but no news of Lord Cranborne. Lord
Salisbury made constant excuses for going out on to the steps. He was
far more nervous than she [Lady Salisbury] was. The Americans arrived
and we proceeded to lunch, and were halfway through before the
telegram arrived. Lord Salisbury read it and simply said, 'Bad news from
Darwen [where Cranborne was standing as a candidate], we have lost it

by 200.' Lady Salisbury at the other end of the table saw something was wrong, but as she was listening to a story she could not ask the news for some minutes. When at last the telegram was passed to her, she read it out and said in the calmest voice, 'Oh, that is a great bore.' And Linky [Hugh Cecil, another of the Salisburys' sons], who was sitting next her, said, 'Very tiresome!' They were wonderful, though you could see how much they both felt it, he especially. There was a sickening silence for a few minutes. I very nearly burst into tears. Several batches of telegrams arrived after that, most of them losses, but nothing seemed to matter after that. What Lord Salisbury feels most is the ingratitude of the country. I long to throw myself on the ground and kiss his feet, I feel such an admiration for him. I feel that this election has so stirred me up, and especially this day, that I shall take an interest in politics ever after. I never realised before the overwhelming interest of them. Con says Lady Salisbury had a good breakdown afterwards, which must have done her good, for she behaved in a marvellous way.

I think this house is perfectly lovely and really luxurious. All the same, nothing would induce me to live here. It was rather funny last night when we went to the drawing-room. Lord Salisbury seized up a candle and lit the fire. Lady Salisbury rushed to the window and threw it wide open. When Lord Salisbury perceived this, though, he soon shut it again. I was very glad, for it was bitterly cold. Linky said that when Lord Salisbury opened the telegram announcing Jim's defeat, he first turned sick, and thought he should faint, and afterwards got the giggles at the sight of the Lytton family all wondering what they should say next.

By November 1892, when she stayed at Hatfield again, Lady Emily's ability to keep her end up in dinner-table conversation had improved.

My dinner last night was very alarming and yet very funny. I sat between Lord Cranborne, whom I think perfectly charming, and Linky, who was here for one night and who makes me feel terribly shy. The conversation was so funny I must tell it you in the order it came. Headaches, pretty women, dogs, music, poetry, painting, sculpture, waxworks, and finally tortures. Breakfast is almost the worst meal of the day, for there are little tables spread about and you may get caught by some alarming person. Con says she was once in an awful situation, having begun a table by herself when Lord Salisbury came in and felt obliged to sit by her, and they talked about *jam*. Con says this was the most awful moment of her life.

Whatever the hiccups in the career of his eldest son, Lord Salisbury's nephew, Arthur James Balfour, excelled in the political arena, both as an effective Irish Secretary and as Leader of the House of Commons for his uncle, whose title confined him to the House of Lords. In his spare time, when not playing tennis, golfing or bicycling, Balfour wrote philosophical works. Margot Asquith, whose husband H. H. Asquith was Liberal Prime Minister from 1908 to 1916, is qualified in her praise of him, writing in 1920.

He was difficult to understand, because I was never sure that he needed me, and difficult to know intimately, because of his formidable detachment. The most that many of us could hope for was that he had a taste in us as one might have in clocks or china.

Mr Balfour was blessed or cursed at his birth, according to individual opinion, by two assets: charm and wits. The disadvantage of charm—which makes me say cursed or blessed—is that it inspires everyone to combine and smooth the way for you throughout life. As the earnest housemaid removes dust, so all his friends and relations kept disagreeable things from his path; and this gave him more leisure in his life than anyone ought to have.

His wits, with which I say that he was also cursed or blessed—quite apart from his brains—gave him confidence in his improvisings and the power to sustain any opinion on any subject, whether he held the opinion or not, with equal brilliance, plausibility and success, according to his desire to dispose of you or the subject. He either finessed with the ethical basis of his intellect, or had none. This made him unintelligible to the average man, unforgivable to the fanatic and a god to the blunderer.

On one occasion my husband and I went to a lunch to meet Mr Frank Harris.* [He], in a general disquisition to the table, at last turned to Arthur Balfour and said, with an air of finality: 'The fact is, Mr Balfour, all the faults of the age come from Christianity and journalism.'

To which Arthur replied with rapier quickness and a child-like air: 'Christianity, of course . . . but why journalism?'

When men said, which they have done now for over thirty years, that Arthur Balfour was too much of a philosopher to be really interested in politics, I always contradicted them. With his intellectual taste, perfect literary style and keen interest in philosophy and religion, nothing but a great love of politics could account for his not having given up more of his time to writing. People thought that he was not interested because he had nothing active in his political aspirations; he saw nothing that needed changing. Low wages, drink, disease, sweating and overcrowding did not concern him; they left him cold and he had not the power to

* A lively journalist, fabricator and scoundrel, famous for his autobiography *My Lives and Loves*.

express a moral indignation which he was too detached to feel. He was a great Parliamentarian, a brilliant debater and a famous Irish Secretary in difficult times, but his political energies lay in tactics. He took a Puck-like pleasure in watching the game of party politics, not in the interests of any particular political party, nor from *esprit de corps*, but from taste.

Politicians from opposing parties would meet at the receptions and country house parties given by the great political hostesses remembered here by Lady Warwick:

From the time I married, down to the era of the Great War, these hostesses were a dominant factor in English politics. They had vast resources, had been trained almost from birth in the art of entertaining, and were excellent judges of character. They provided, in town or country, a rendezvous where men of all shades of opinion—provided the shades were not too deep or too discordant—might meet to discuss the affairs of the session and the day.

They exercised their power largely through their pull over their own sex. A man might start his political career with every intention of being independent; he might set out to annoy the Government, to embarrass ministers, to give trouble of every sort and kind, in the fashion that a skilled parliamentarian can. But if he proved too difficult, there were many ways of bringing him to heel, and the most effective was by cutting him off from the social centre! This might not matter to him, but it mattered terribly to his wife and daughters, who could be counted upon to bring domestic pressure to bear.

Always ready to entertain on behalf of the party, [a political hostess] would make her reception rooms the rendezvous of a thousand strivers. Her country house was the meeting-place of men who ridiculed or reviled each other in Parliament, yet were on the best of terms when the curtain fell upon the perennial farce. Because she knew everybody who was anybody, she was able to collect under her roof the most diverse interests, and there reconcile them.

Entertainment among the élite was undoubtedly an art. The enchantment lay in setting us at ease in a luxury that was exquisite, without thought of cost. Here, in an atmosphere of beauty, men and women reposed; even statesmen lost their stateliness, and surrendered to delicate suggestion. Petticoat influence!

In writing of the years between 1880 and 1906, it can be said that matters of high importance to the State were constantly decided between Liberals and Conservatives in the country houses of England. As time went on, it became necessary to extend the limits of social intercourse,

for politicians of the more violent kind began to make a name for themselves. They found that doors hitherto barred were opening automatically. I remember the amazement at Chatsworth when the Duke of Devonshire (*plus royaliste que le roi*) announced at luncheon that he was expecting Mr Joseph Chamberlain for the weekend. The Radical from Birmingham, one of the outer barbarians, to storm the ducal door! I recall someone asking me if I thought he would know how to conduct himself with outward decency. She prophesied gloomily that he would eat peas with his knife, since anything was possible to a demagogue. That evening Mr Chamberlain must have reassured the doubting one. His calm appraisement of the company, his dignified appreciation of the atmosphere, established him immediately as someone with whom even great hostesses would have to reckon.*

The real aim and purpose of the great hostesses was to maintain the *status quo*. They wanted to make things easy for both sides, so that while Whig and Tory, Liberal and Conservative, wrangled across the floor of the House, there was always an opportunity for social intercourse between the acts. Thus they combined to protect themselves, as far as they could, against legislative changes which might militate against the interests of the class to which both belonged.

In spite of invitations being restricted to friends and acquaintances, 500 was no large figure for a political reception, which would start at nine o'clock in the evening and be over at midnight. Supper would be an affair of the buffet, but would be of irreproachable quality. There were no sterner critics of champagne, *foie gras*, quail, and the rest of the familiar luxuries, than the people who attended receptions. The kümmel had to be of the same country as its concomitant — the caviare.

Few women could give both classes of reception, the political and the social. Theresa, Lady Londonderry, was one of these. She was an exception to the general rule of limitation, as indeed she was to most other rules. She was older than I, and though we were very friendly, we were never sufficiently intimate for me to see her unbend, though there must have been occasions when the softer side of her nature showed itself, or she would not have had so many admirers. Outwardly hard and unapproachable, she was yet the most wonderful hostess.

Lansdowne House was a favourite resort of the politicians and their followings. It had a wonderful setting, and Lady Lansdowne possessed a flair for entertainment. The Duchess of Buccleuch, at Montagu House, received only the most exclusive circle in London. Society for her

* This must have been shortly after the Duke, as the head of other Liberal Unionists, abandoned Gladstone and his Home Rule policy. Chamberlain led the Radical Unionists.

Arthur Balfour,
by Sir Lawrence Alma-Tadema

Lady Londonderry as the Empress Maria Theresa, at the Duchess of Devonshire's fancy dress ball for the 1897 Jubilee (see p. 226)

Lady Tweedmouth as Queen Elizabeth I, and her husband as the Earl of Leicester

consisted only of those upon whom she permitted herself to smile. The unfavoured were all of the outer darkness.

When Lord Salisbury was Prime Minister, a reception at the Foreign Office, with Lady Salisbury as hostess, was incomparably splendid, dazzling both to the eye and to the mind. It was certain that some of the royal family would attend. Rajahs and Maharajahs, ambassadors and foreign attachés in uniforms of infinite splendour, stalked god-like among the stately beauties of St James's. Ablaze with jewels and the sashes of countless orders, they glowed with colour and complacency.

Brook House, Park Lane, when Lady Tweedmouth ruled, had wonderful rooms, but, like the Spencers at Spencer House, her political gatherings were limited to the Liberals. I am compelled to state that they were not as ornate as those at the other houses. I cannot understand why the Liberal party has never been able to give as splendid entertainments as its Conservative rivals, but the fact remains.

It was a costly business to give political receptions. It was necessary to spend at least five hundred pounds to entertain five hundred people, even in those far-off days when a pound was actually worth twenty shillings. It was not the buffet supper that was so expensive, although it was of the best, because prices were comparatively reasonable in those days. The main outlay was on floral decorations. There was a great rage for this, and each hostess tried to outvie her friends. The great masses of flowers made the rooms look wonderful, but I always thought there were two things against them. In the first place, the scent was overpowering, and had a very definite effect upon delicate women—most professional singers know that it damages the voice. In the second place, it seemed tragic to destroy so much beauty for the sake of a few hours—when the reception was over most of the flowers had withered.

Lady Warwick

'Society'

In late Victorian England the upper ranks of the leisured classes were very much in thrall to the demands and conventions of Society, for sound reasons of self-preservation. The motions that Society went through each year in London, and at one or two select racecourses, made up the Season, which lasted from spring until late July. Young girls who were being introduced to it, and its associated marriage market, were said to be 'coming out', and had to be presented at Court, at one of the royal 'Drawing Rooms'. Lady Warwick sets out some of the ground rules, then G. W. E. Russell has some fun at the expense of aristocratic titles.

Lady Warwick

When I came out, social prestige meant something. There was a definite aristocratic society of the landowning families. These families owned then practically the whole of the land of England. It was difficult to enter that society from the outside, and impossible unless royalty approved. The Prince of Wales was broadish-minded and inclined to welcome some of the professional class. A few artists and doctors were accepted. Sometimes a rich manufacturer might be able to poke his nose in, but he caught it for his temerity no matter how rich he might be. Political people were included, and any outstanding man or woman, say an explorer or a musician, but brains were rarely appreciated and literary people and intellectuals were not welcome. As for newspaper men, their entry was unheard of. Society did not want to be made to think.

G. W. E. Russell

Every constitutional Briton, whatever his political creed, has in his heart of hearts a wholesome reverence for a dukedom. As, according to Dr Johnson, all claret would be port if it could, so, presumably, every marquis would like to be a duke; and yet, as a matter of fact, that Elysian translation is seldom made. A marquis, properly regarded, is not so much a nascent duke as an amplified earl. A shrewd observer of the world once said to me: 'When an earl gets a marquisate, it is worth a hundred thousand pounds in hard money to his family.' The explanation of this cryptic utterance is that, whereas an earl's younger sons are 'misters', a marquis's younger sons are 'lords'. Each 'my lord' can make a 'my lady', and therefore commands a distinctly higher price in the marriage market of a wholesomely-minded community. Miss Higgs, with her fifty thousand pounds, might scorn the notion of becoming the Honourable Mrs Percy Popjoy; but as Lady Magnus Charters she would feel a laudable ambition gratified.

An earldom is, in its combination of euphony, antiquity, and association, perhaps the most impressive of all the titles in the peerage. But the children of an earl are the half-castes of the peerage. The eldest son is 'my lord', and his sisters are 'my lady'; but the younger sons are not distinguishable from the ignominious progeny of viscounts and barons. Two little boys, respectively the eldest and the second son of an earl, were playing on the front staircase of their home, when the eldest fell over into the hall below. The younger called to the footman who picked his brother up, 'Is he hurt?' 'Killed, *my lord*,' was the instantaneous reply of a servant who knew the devolution of a courtesy title.

As the marquesses people the debatable land between the dukes and the earls, so do the viscounts between the earls and the barons. A child whom Matthew Arnold was examining in grammar once wrote of certain words which he found it hard to classify under their proper parts of speech that they were 'thrown into the common sink, which is adverbs'. I hope I shall not be considered guilty of any disrespect if I say that ex-Speakers, ex-Secretaries of State, successful generals, and ambitious barons who are not quite good enough for earldoms, are 'thrown into the common sink, which is viscounts'.

After viscounts, barons. The baronage of England is headed by the bishops; it is held on good authority that no human being ever experiences a rapture so intense as an American bishop from a western state when he first hears himself called 'My lord' at a London dinner party. After the spiritual barons come the secular barons—the 'common or garden' peers of the United Kingdom. Of these there are considerably more than three hundred; and of all, except some thirty or forty at the most, it may be said without offence that they are products of the opulent middle class. Pitt destroyed deliberately and for ever the exclusive character of the British peerage when, as Lord Beaconsfield said, he 'created a plebeian aristocracy and blended it with the patrician oligarchy'. And in order to gain admission to this 'plebeian aristocracy' men otherwise reasonable and honest will spend incredible sums,

48

undergo prodigious exertions, associate themselves with the basest intrigues, and perform the most unblushing tergiversations. Lord Houghton* told me that he said to a well-known politician who boasted that he had refused a peerage: 'Then you made a great mistake. A peerage would have secured you three things that you are much in need of—social consideration, longer credit with your tradesmen, and better marriages for your younger children.'

What is a baronet? ask some. Sir Wilfrid Lawson† (who ought to know) replies that he is a man 'who has ceased to be a gentleman and has not become a nobleman'. But this is too severe a judgement. It breathes a spirit of contempt bred of familiarity, which may, without irreverence, be assumed by a member of an exalted order, but which a humble outsider would do well to avoid.

E. F. Benson gives a vignette of a fine example of a duke, he of Devonshire.

While he was still in the House of Commons as Lord Hartington he became one of the most powerful units of influence there, not because he was possessed of any very exceptional genius or had great political dexterity or because he was personally ambitious. Indeed it was exactly because he was indifferent to personal motives, because he had no enthusiasms (the happiest moment of his life, he was reported to have said, was when his pig took a first prize at some agricultural show) that [his wife] saw what a tremendous force he could become. He had no axe to grind, and that was why he could deliver such stunning blows with it. His bitterest opponents could not accuse him of self-seeking, because it was obvious that he wanted nothing for himself, for the man who in the course of nature will become Duke of Devonshire and inherit colossal wealth and noble possessions has not very much that he can covet for himself among the vain trappings of the material world. So when, with his great position and very sound judgement, he made up his mind (which took time) on any political question, it was because he thought that such a course was right, and probity, when all is said and done, is the most valuable equipment in any career. Sometimes when he was in office he had to stand up and make a statement of policy, uninspired always, but full of plain common sense, and always to be listened to as the conviction of a perfectly honest man with regard to the welfare of his country. No wizardry of speech, no sophistically attractive argument liable to be torn to shreds, no ridicule of his opponents, in the modern mode, gave spice to these laborious pronouncements; once he yawned heavily

* Richard Monckton Milnes, created Baron Houghton in 1863.
† Baronet and Radical MP.

in the middle of a statement, and accounted for this lapse by explaining that what he was saying 'was so damned dull'. He found it so himself, and that was partly why it was impressive.

'Tiny', daughter of Sir Mountstuart Grant Duff, Governor of Madras, was presented at Court in 1888.

We went up [to London] in February and my mother took me to Cresser [then the 'in' dress designer] to choose my Drawing-Room dress: though presentations at Court were then held in the daytime and in the Palace Drawing Room (instead of the Ballroom), full evening dress was worn. Mr Cresser looked me over calmly for a moment or two in complete silence, and then said, 'I think a *ceinture sauvage* ['tribal' belt] would suit Miss Grant Duff.' My mother gasped, for it sounded as though there were to be nothing else. But he made a lovely dress of white satin, covered with white chiffon and ornamented with a *ceinture sauvage* in pearls around the hips and another around the bodice.

I forget what minor royalty died that winter, but I seized on the opportunity of court mourning to procure for myself a slinky frock of black and a hat of similar hue with a falling lace veil that completely covered my face. Seeing me in it for the first time, Lady Sligo asked why I chose to appear as a lovely French widow. Lady Sligo was at that time one of the most charming hostesses in London and one of the wittiest women I ever met. She had that extraordinary logic and common sense which are perhaps the most remarkable gift of the French. Always amusing, she also showed a great sense of justice and benevolence.

I remember my first visit to her, a very shy child of eighteen. She turned to my mother and said, 'Julia, I hope she flirts.' My mother said firmly that she hoped I did not. Lady Sligo's response was to turn to me and say, 'My dear, do not in this matter listen to your mother. If you do not flirt you will never know what sort of man you will want to marry.' On another occasion a certain great lady was bemoaning that her son should want to marry a nobody, whereupon Lady Sligo leaned fatly across their intervening chairs and, slapping her on the knee, said, 'My dear, if nobody married nobodies where would you and I be?'

We were always at home on Sundays, and endless men came to call. There was a rite about this, as there was about everything else, and the man who was intimate enough to leave his hat in the hall felt superior to the man who had to carry up his hat and wrestle with it and his gloves and his teacup. The rule was, roughly, that if you were alone with your hostess and her girl, and another man turned up, you could stay because the ratio would be two to two, but if you were with your hostess alone and

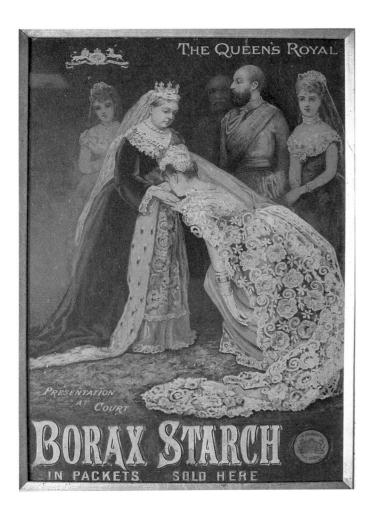

A débutante trying hard not to let her nose touch the Queen's hand while being presented at a royal 'Drawing Room'

no one else came, you were supposed to leave at the end of ten minutes.

No one danced during Lent, but there were a good many quiet dinner and evening parties, and my first Drawing Room. It was a terrible ordeal, and made worse by taking place in the morning. It requires courage to face one's sovereign almost naked at twelve noon on a wintry day. Upon arrival in the presence of Her Majesty, young men in uniform seized our four-yard trains and pulled them out; we realised we had to make five curtseys and withdraw backwards before they would be safely tucked up on our arms again. I knew that what the Queen disliked most was having the back of her hand knocked by the lady's nose as she arose from her curtsey, and my agony was such that I almost fainted with terror. But I managed not to touch the august hand with my nose. The Prince of Wales shook hands with my mother and me and we then backed out.

One of the other Royal contributions to the Season was the Buckingham Palace Garden Party. In 1889 Sir Henry Ponsonby reported the suggestion of Lord Ritchie that 'the Queen should throw open Buckingham

51

The Queen at the Diamond Jubilee Garden Party in the grounds of Buckingham Palace, as described by Lady Monkswell on p. 226. Painting by Laurits Tuxen

Palace Gardens, when she is not there, to the public. I told him he might as well ask her to dance the fandango.' So the only chance of seeing them was a Garden Party invitation, which Lady Monkswell received in 1896.

It was a wonderful function, five or six thousand people, the thermometer standing at 86° in the shade. It is a revelation to get inside those garden walls of Buckingham Palace, the outside of which we know so well. The moment I was inside I felt a different creature. At once you come upon a charming little gardener's house and shady walks. In sixty or seventy yards you come to the edge of the ornamental water, then more shady walks and the great lawn opens before you, with the Palace looking very fine with its huge terrace in front. Now I pause to remember it must indeed have been an interesting party as we were there from four-thirty to past seven and were never dull at all. The place was thronged but there was no crowd. I spoke to some fifty people, and my brain goes round to think of all the lovely muslin dresses the girls wore and the unspeakable hats. Whilst I was sitting just outside the tent, I looked up and beheld Mrs Bayard, the American Minister's wife, leaning upon the arm of Oliver Holmes.* I was delighted to see him and walked with him

* Mr Justice Holmes, son of Oliver Wendell Holmes, the essayist.

right through the grounds up to the Constitution Hill Gate. Mr Bayard too treated me with great distinction. Afterwards I watched the royal party, [as] they worked like galley slaves at talking to people. The Princess of Wales looked very beautiful in a lilac suit, the Duchess of York [the future Queen Mary] very smart and well set up; Princess Christian very square and stout.

When we first came in the water-men in their red liveries and black velvet hunting caps, and a little fleet of eight or ten boats were the most striking object. I resolved that if possible I would have a row. Just before seven I secured Bob and we walked down to the little landing place and got into a boat, rather childish of me but I think it was the prettiest ten minutes of the afternoon. I saw Lord Salisbury looking smarter than he ever appears in the House of Lords, old Joe Chamberlain and his pretty American wife, George Curzon and his pretty [American] wife talking to Irving the actor, the Duchess of Marlborough [Consuelo Vanderbilt] in yellow muslin, and the lovely Duchess of Portland in white.

Lady Warwick recorded that 'the Victorians of my little world regarded food with an interest and an enthusiasm that has no counterpart today'. (She was writing in about 1930.) Her somewhat random comments expand on this. Then Tiny Grant Duff tells how she and her friends coped with the tedium of long dinners, and E. F. Benson recalls a famous gourmet, Harry Chaplin. In one guise, he was the epitome of the old English squire; in another, a famous figure of the Turf and crony of the Prince of Wales.

Lady Warwick

You could take it as a rule that the larger the house, and the more numerous the flunkeys, the worse would be the food. Perhaps this was due in no small measure to the distance between kitchens and dining-rooms in those great mansions that have now fallen on evil days.

There were all sorts of rules governing dinners. For example, if you had more than twelve guests, there must be, in addition to two soups and two kinds of fish, etc., two entrées, of which one must be brown and one white. Quails were very popular. I have been at many a dance-supper at which the number of guests ran into three figures, yet every guest had a quail.

I think it was the introduction of cigarette smoking immediately after dinner by the Prince of Wales that killed the claret habit in London. After the first whiff or two it was difficult to tell good wine from bad, and champagne speedily took the place of Bordeaux. Men began to follow

Christmas dinner

the example set by the Prince, of leaving the dining-table almost immediately after dinner to join the ladies.

Tiny Grant Duff

We used to amuse ourselves by betting on whether the guests opposite would eat all the dinner. Whosoever's protégé ate the most won the stakes. I remember a terrible episode once when, getting very excited because my old gentleman was not eating well and seeing him pass the sweet, I leaned forward and begged him to have some. He happened to be the Dean of Westminster. The whole table stopped talking and watched and could not imagine why I was so impertinent. I, of course, got scarlet, and my poor neighbour was convulsed. The Dean said, 'It is very kind of you, my dear young lady, but I am not so young as you are.' My mother was very cross. We invented a great many dodges for making dull people talk. I am supposed to have coined the immortal question, 'Do you like string?' And I think it was I who invented the alphabet game, in which one began, say, 'Do you like apples?' and had to get the conversation to badminton or the Balearic Isles without being observed. One made round pellets of bread for each letter achieved.

54

Harry Chaplin placed high among the pleasures of the table, as every true gourmet does, victuals of plain perfection. Lady Radnor [Chaplin's sister] and he and I were once strolling after lunch on Sunday in her kitchen-garden at Cookham, and he observed a fine row of broad beans. 'My dear,' he said to her, 'those look excellent beans. Do tell your gardener to send some into the house and let us have beans and bacon for dinner. There's nothing in the world so good.' The gardener was off duty, as it was Sunday afternoon, but she said that if he cared to pick them and bring them to the house, he should have his dish. So off came his hat, and we filled it with the bean-pods, and carried it in triumph to the cook, and Mr Harry said that he would have beans and bacon for dinner, and nothing else whatever; he could not imagine a more delicious dinner. But then the gourmet had a word to say to that, for when dinner-time came, he first refused soup, but then discovered that it had the most attractive aroma, and said he would just have 'a spoonful of soup', which meant an ordinary helping for a grown man. Some fish was then placed before him, and he ate his fish in an absent-minded manner, almost mournfully in fact, for it was salmon, and it reminded him of a heavy fish he had lost on the Brora [a Scottish river]. Then, so suitably for this hot evening, there was some cold pressed beef (for he remembered how excellent his sister's pressed beef always was), and a mouthful of chicken. Then naturally he must eat the beans and bacon which had been provided specially for him, and so he had two helpings of them and said he had never tasted such excellent beans and the bacon was very good too. Where did she get it? . . . A very pleasant custom of his, if the dish was remarkable and he made a second attack on it, was to put a sovereign on the edge of it, to be given, with his compliments, to the cook. Dinner was a serious matter demanding his entire attention: his neighbour in the middle of that function, alluding to the famous *boiseries* [panelling] of the dining-room where they were sitting, once said to him 'What beautiful carving!' And naturally he replied, 'Yes, the service is always very good in this house.'

The standards expected of young women within Society were very different from those for young men, even if, as Tiny Grant Duff claimed, it was possible to give one's chaperone the slip for a bit. 'When we came out we were told that we must not dance more than three or four times with the same man, but all the same we managed quite comfortably to get in eight or nine whirls with one partner whilst our chaperones were down at supper or

55

Arrangement in Black No. 5: Lady
Meux, *by James McNeill Whistler.
Valerie Meux was a walking example of
the exclusivity of Society. She had worked
under the name of Val Reece at the Casino
de Venise in Holborn before catching
her husband, scion of a wealthy brewing
family. Even though she wrote to his grandmother, the Marchioness of Aylesbury
(see p.63), that 'my sins were committed
before marriage and not after', she was
never accepted by the upper classes*

*talking to elderly friends in corners.' Lady Warwick explains the other side
of the coin.*

I remember smart young men about town who had no profession other
than perhaps soldiering, and to my mind soldiering makes for stagna-
tion. The Blues and the Guards mostly supplied London ballrooms
with eligibles. Society girls, if not as innocent as they were 'pure', were
often unbelievably ignorant even of the physical facts of marriage. Marriage—their goal, their destiny, their desire—was all in a rosy haze.
Afterwards, as wives, they accepted without question the code of their
day as unchanging and unchangeable. Nearly all the young men had mis-
tresses, so most bridegrooms had a second establishment to pension off
or maintain. The only thing that mattered was that there should be no
scandal; everything was all right if only it was kept quiet, hushed up, covered. If a Society woman met a man—even her own brother—in the park
or in a restaurant, when he was accompanied by his mistress or an
actress, he would not raise his hat to her. He cut her, and she understood.

Anthony Hope, author of The Prisoner of Zenda, *is remembered today as the inventor of Ruritania, but his first real success was with* The Dolly Dialogues *in 1894, a series of linked pieces, the narrator of which has recently lost the hand of Miss Dolly Foster to the Earl of Mickleham. They have a Wildean flavour to them and give us a taste of what it was to be a young gentleman of leisure in the Nineties.*

Old Lady M. sent for me the other day. I had not the honour of knowing the Countess, and I went in some trepidation. When I was ushered in, Lady Mickleham put up her 'starers'. (You know those abominations! *Pince-nez* with long torture—I mean tortoise—shell handles.)

'Mr—er—Carter?' said she.

I bowed. I would have denied it if I could.

'My dears!' said Lady Mickleham.

Upon this five young ladies who had been sitting in five straight-backed chairs, doing five pieces of embroidery, rose, bowed, and filed out of the room. I felt very nervous. A pause followed. Then the Countess observed—and it seemed at first rather irrelevant—

'I've been reading an unpleasant story.'

'In these days of French influence,' I began apologetically (not that I write such stories, or indeed any stories, but Lady Mickleham invites an apologetic attitude), and my eye wandered to the table. I saw nothing worse (or better) than the morning paper there.

'Contained in a friend's letter,' she continued, focusing the 'starers' full on my face.

I did not know what to do, so I bowed again.

'It must have been as painful for her to write as for me to read,' Lady Mickleham went on. 'And that is saying much. Be seated, pray.'

I bowed, and sat down in one of the straight-backed chairs. I also began, in my fright, to play with one of the pieces of embroidery.

'Is Lady Jane's work in your way?'

I dropped the embroidery, and put my foot on my hat.

'I believe, Mr Carter, that you are acquainted with Miss Dorothea Foster?'

'I have that pleasure,' said I.

'Who is about to be married to my son, the Earl of Mickleham?'

'That, I believe, is so,' said I. I was beginning to pull myself together.

'My son, Mr Carter, is of a simple and trusting disposition. Perhaps I had better come to the point. I am informed by this letter that, in conversation with the writer the other day, Archibald mentioned, quite incidentally, some very startling facts. Those facts concern you, Mr Carter.'

'May I ask the name of the writer?'

'I do not think that is necessary,' said she. 'She is a lady in whom I have the utmost confidence.'

'That is, of course, enough,' said I.

'It appears, Mr Carter—and you will excuse me if I speak plainly—(I set my teeth) that you have, in the first place, given to my son's bride a wedding present, which I can only describe as——'

'A pearl ornament,' I interposed; 'with a ruby or two, and——'

'A pearl heart,' she corrected; 'er—fractured, and that you explained that this absurd article represented your heart.'

'Mere *badinage*,' said I.

'In execrably bad taste,' said she.

I bowed.

'In fact, most offensive. But that is not the worst. From my son's further statements it appears that on one occasion, at least, he found you and Miss Foster engaged in what I can only call——'

I raised my hand in protest. The Countess took no notice.

'What I can only call *romping*.'

She shot this word at me with extraordinary violence, and when it was out she shuddered.

'Romping!' I cried.

'A thing not only atrociously vulgar at all times, but under the circumstances—need I say more? Mr Carter, you were engaged in chasing my son's future bride round a table!'

'Pardon me, Lady Mickleham. Your son's future bride was engaged in chasing me round a table.'

'It is the same thing,' said Lady Mickleham.

'I should have thought there was a distinction,' said I.

'None at all.'

I fell back on a second line of defence.

'I didn't let her catch me, Lady Mickleham,' I pleaded.

Lady Mickleham grew quite red. This made me feel more at my ease.

'No, sir. If you had——'

'Goodness knows!' I murmured, shaking my head.

'As it happened, however, my son entered in the middle of this disgraceful——'

'It was at the beginning,' said I, with a regretful sigh.

Upon this—and I have really never been so pleased at anything in all my life—the Countess, the violence of her emotions penetrating to her very fingers, gripped the handle of her 'starers' with such force that she broke it in two! She was a woman of the world, and in a moment she looked as if nothing had happened. With me it was different; and that I am not now on Lady Mickleham's visiting-list is due to (*inter alia et*

enormia) the fact that I laughed! It was out before I could help it. In a second I was as grave as a mute. The mischief was done. The Countess rose. I imitated her example.

'You are amused?' said she, and her tones banished the last of my mirth. I stumbled on my hat, and it rolled to her feet.

'It is not probable,' she observed, 'that after Miss Foster's marriage you will meet her often. You will move in—er—somewhat different circles.'

'I may catch a glimpse of her in her carriage from the top of my 'bus' said I.

'Your *milieu* and my son's——'

'I know his valet, though,' said I.

Lady Mickleham rang the bell. I stooped for my hat. To tell the truth I was rather afraid to expose myself in such a defenceless attitude, but the Countess preserved her self-control. The butler opened the door. I bowed, and left the Countess regarding me through the maimed 'starers'. Then I found the butler smiling. He probably knew the signs of the weather. I wouldn't be Lady Mickleham's butler if you made me a duke.

As I walked home through the Park I met Miss Dolly and Mickleham. They stopped. I walked on. Mickleham seized me by the coat-tails.

'Do you mean to cut us?' he cried.

Le Mariage de convenance, *by Sir William Orchardson. A marvellously atmospheric late Victorian narrative painting with the boredom of the young wife made palpable*

59

*The formidable
Louise, Duchess of
Manchester, and
later of Devonshire*

'Yes,' said I.

'Why, what the deuce?' he began.

'I've seen your mother,' said I. 'I wish, Mickleham, that when you do happen to intrude as you did the other day, you wouldn't repeat what you see.'

'Lord!' he cried. 'She's not heard of that? I only told Aunt Cynthia.'

I said something about Aunt Cynthia.

'Does—does she know it *all*?' asked Miss Dolly.

The Dowager Countess of Mickleham sounds like a soulmate of Wilde's Lady Bracknell, but both might have met their match in the 'Double Duchess', Louise von Alten, who was married to the Duke of Manchester before she became the Duchess of Devonshire. E. F. Benson describes her, and then the Countess de Grey, a much more sympathetic figure, who entertained with what Benson calls a touch of 'apotheosised Bohemianism'.

Most people found the Duchess of Devonshire rather formidable, for she could be unexpectedly ruthless in her ways. They never quite knew, and so they were careful. One day a couple of young men drove over to lunch with her at Bolton Abbey [a Yorkshire property of the Devonshires]. Afterwards she drove them out in a wagonette with a pair of horses to see the Strid, where the River Wharfe bustles down, swift and deep, between narrow rocks. It was raining, a cheerless day, but she would like a breath of air, and she carried no umbrella, only a stick. As she was getting back again into the wagonette, after having majestically observed the Strid, one of the horses moved on a step, then was checked again, and she was thrown forward on to her knees in the carriage. With-

61

out a word she hit her coachman smartly over the back with her stick, and then seating herself said to her companions, 'As I was just saying ——' On another occasion, when there was some rumour about that Devonshire House was to be sold, a friend, rather imprudently, asked her if it was true. She said very drily: 'Yes, perfectly true. We are proposing to live at Clapham Junction instead. So convenient a train service.'

The Countess de Grey was very tall, a full six feet, but of so matchless a grace that the effect was not that she looked tall, but that most other women looked squat. It was the last night of the opera season, and Edouard and Jean de Reszke [famous opera singers] came on to a little party [at her smallish house in Mayfair]. There were not more than fifty guests all told, the Duke of Cambridge [the Queen's cousin] was among them, and he, sitting on a very low chair, was sunk in the condition which hypnotists call 'light trance'; not asleep, at least not at all sound asleep, but slightly oblivious to external impressions. Then Alick Yorke [an epicene courtier] came tripping in, with a little rouge and an eyebrow and a stupendous carnation in his button-hole; he was not much more than five feet tall. He looked up at his hostess who had done her hair in some amazing manner, piling it on the top of her head, while somewhere near the summit was a diamond crescent; indeed for once she looked almost too tall. Alick Yorke surveyed her critically, blinked up at the crescent, and with a little lisp he said, 'Dear Gladys, I like the way you've done your hair tonight. It gives you what you've always wanted— height.' Oscar Wilde came drifting largely along, and caught sight of some new arrival. 'Oh, I'm so glad you've come,' he said. 'There are a hundred things I want not to say to you.' Then Réjane [an actress] recited 'La Poupée', and after a few trifles of that kind, all rather informally bestowed, Lady de Grey, purely for a joke, said to Edouard de Reszke, 'Won't you sing something?' He, instead of answering her according to her folly and saying he hadn't brought his music, said, 'But certainly I will, though I have never sung in so small a room. I will sing you "Le Veau d'Or" from *Faust*.' He had a prodigious volume of voice when he chose to open it out, and now he sang 'Le Veau d'Or' as loud as he possibly could, and the windows rattled, and the crystal festoons of the chandelier quivered. He sang it with extravagant operatic gestures, parodying himself, with an eye all the time on the Duke of Cambridge, but he never disturbed the light trance. And then Jean de Reszke, fired by this noble exhibition, and slightly jealous, said, 'But I want to sing too. I will show you how I sing the "Preis-lied".' So he found two footstools and placed them in the middle of the room, and insecurely perched on them proceeded also to parody himself. He sang it as he

62

always sang it, but with some absurd exaggeration of gesture and caricature of the way he took his high notes. Never was anything quite so ludicrous, and before he had finished his singing there was not, quite in the
Victorian manner, a dry eye in the room except those of the Duke of
Cambridge . . . Bohemia in excelsis: Bohemia in tiaras.

Maria, Marchioness of Aylesbury, was another original grande dame, *as
remembered by Lady Warwick. This and the following extract, also by
Lady Warwick, testify to the importance of Hyde Park within Society's
scheme of things.*

She wore her hair parted, with a lot of small corkscrew curls on either
side, and this gave her a quaint old-world aspect. She was a very practical
woman, with rigid views on the question of hospitality.

'Never forget, dear,' she would say to me, ' "a chop for a chop"—that
is the rule of entertainment, in town—or if it isn't, it should be.'

I once drove with her in the Park in the afternoon, and for some time I
was astonished at the number of passing carriages to which she would
make a slight stately inclination, in return for a respectful salute from
coachman or footman. I thought I knew a good many people, but I was
nowhere with Lady A., and at last I told her so.

'My dear,' she explained, 'there are a lot of those people whom I do
not know; but I have trained a great number of footmen and coachmen,
and they are grateful to me—as they should be.'

In the Eighties and Nineties there was only *one* Park, called Hyde. We
knew dimly of Regent's Park as a place where the Zoo existed, as we discovered Battersea when the cycling craze was on [see p. 129]. St James's
and the Green Park were a short cut to the House of Lords, but when we
spoke of 'the Park' it was always Hyde Park near the Corner. Here the
small circle of Society with the big 'S' was sure of meeting all its members on morning ride or drive, or in the late afternoon between tea and
dinner, in what was practically a daily Society garden party! Sometimes,
engaged couples or the partners of illicit assignations wandered as far as
the Serpentine banks, but there they were liable to meet 'Bayswater' and
'the people who rowed on the water', and all soon shuddered back to the
inviolate spot. In the late Nineties 'Bayswater'—no other suburb was
known—invaded the Society Church Parade on a Sunday morning, but
these interlopers had scant welcome, and the little Society ranks closed
up only the more exclusively by the Achilles statue.

I remember the noon daily drive of my phaeton with high-stepping
chestnuts, or browns, or bays, eagerly recognised by admiring friends

who crowded round on horseback or on foot when one pulled up at the entrance to the Row* and chatted of the social round—of future meetings, of dances, lunches, and dinners within 'the Circle'. My horses were so well known that they always made a stir. One 'booked' friends for luncheon, and perhaps drove them down Piccadilly prancing on the wide sweep of pavement, glancing up at the Turf Club window as a possible place to find an extra man for a dinner party. If you lived in St James's, as we did, the hill down St James's Street was a splendid show of the 'spanking tits [horses]'; no interfering traffic, and only a hat-raising or bowing to friends hurrying up or down to their luncheon engagements.

Late afternoon in Hyde Park meant state carriages and barouches with beautifully dressed occupants pulled up under the trees. It was not etiquette to handle the reins oneself in afternoons, so we sat on rows of chairs chatting and behaving as if the world we knew bounded by the Smart Set was a fixed orbit, as if London—our London—was a place of select social enjoyment for the Circle, as if nothing could change in this best of delightful worlds. Then there would be a clatter of faster horses, and down this mile of drive came the well-known royal carriage with the beautiful Alexandra, Princess of Wales, bowing right and left as only she could bow, and hats were raised and knees curtsied before seats were resumed and interrupted chatter continued.

An exotic sub-species of Society was spawned early in the Decade of Jubilees—in Arthur Balfour's carefully qualified words, 'a group of friends who have perhaps found a place in English social history'. The nickname of this group, as far as the outside world was concerned, was the Souls; it was bestowed on them by one of the Prince of Wales's breezy friends, Lord Charles Beresford, in 1887 or 88: 'You all sit and talk about each other's souls—I shall call you the Souls.' The name they themselves used was the Gang. Lady Warwick wrote of them: 'This little coterie loved literature and art and perhaps were more pagan than soulful. They were decidedly ambitious, clever, and well-read, and exercised great influence on London society for five or six years. I think they sent us all back to reading more than we otherwise should have done, and this was an excellent thing for us. Indubitably Arthur Balfour was the thinker of the society, a sort of sun—illuminating the subsidiary stars that floated around him.'

Other major figures in this group were George Curzon, who became Viceroy of India in 1898; George Wyndham, later Secretary for Ireland; Harry Cust, who edited the Pall Mall Gazette *in any time he had left over from his relentless philandering; Margot Tennant, who later married H. H. Asquith; Ettie Grenfell, who was to be a great Edwardian hostess; Lady*

---

* Rotten Row, the riding track along the southern side of the Park.

Elcho, chatelaine of one of England's most beautiful houses at Stanway in Gloucestershire, the (probably Platonic) mistress of Arthur Balfour, and sister of George Wyndham; and the beautiful Lady Granby, later Duchess of Rutland and mother of Lady Diana Cooper, thanks to an affair with Harry Cust.

Attempts to see the Souls as a valuable solvent of the rigidities typical of earlier decades, or a timely corrective to the gambling, gourmandising, racing and practical joking of the Prince of Wales's philistine Marlborough House Set, are not entirely convincing. High Victorian religiosity was not replaced in them by any great development of social conscience. In spite of their stress on the cultivation of friendship, the art of conversation and the importance of correspondence, there is a strong whiff of pretension, conceit and mutual admiration pervading the air. Any criticism of the Prince and his friends for wasting their time can be countered by pointing to the ridiculous amount of energy devoted by the Souls to affairs and flirtations between married female members and their various admirers, as well as to elaborate word games, charades and improvisations. In reality, both groups were driven on their ceaseless rounds by the same fear — of boredom. In 1895 Queen Victoria had the last word to say on the Souls, as reported by Marie Mallet, one of her ladies-in-waiting, 'HM said they really ought to be told not *to be so silly!'*

The year before, stirred by reports of some upper-class excess, Field Marshal Lord Wolseley wrote to his wife in all too prophetic words:

To the man whose first thought is England, and who feels that she must sink or be saved by her gentlefolk, the contemplation of English Society is painful. I feel that a country whose upper classes live as a certain set of men and women do, can only be saved from annihilation by some such upheaval as a great war, which will cost all the best families their sons, and call forth both the worst animal passions and the noblest of human virtues, and for the time place the very existence of the kingdom in danger.

The Wyndham Sisters, *by John Singer Sargent. Of these sisters of George Wyndham, Lady Elcho is on the left and Pamela Tennant, married to Margot Asquith's eldest brother, is on the right*

On Strike, *by Sir Hubert von Herkomer*

The Poor

In 1886 Lord Tennyson, the ageing Poet Laureate, wrote a postscript to his poem 'Locksley Hall', and entitled it 'Sixty Years After'. In it he voiced his doubts about the central Victorian belief in Progress and asked a hard-hitting question —

Is it well that while we range with Science, glorying in the Time,
City children soak and blacken soul and sense in city slime?
There among the glooming alleys Progress halts on palsied feet,
Crime and hunger cast our maidens by the thousand on the street.
There the Master scrimps his haggard sempstress of her daily bread,
There a single sordid attic holds the living and the dead.
There the smouldering fire of fever creeps across the rotted floor,
And the crowded couch of incest in the warrens of the poor.

Gladstone, recently ousted from office, had the time to try to answer the question, and in so doing, defend his own record in Government. His article appeared in the January 1887 issue of The Nineteenth Century.

Take first the city child as he is described. For one such child now there were ten, perhaps twenty, fifty years back. A very large, and a still increasing proportion of these children have been brought under the regular training and discipline of the school. Take the maidens, who are now, as they were then, cast by thousands on the street. But then, if one among them were stricken with penitence and sought for a place in which to hide her head, she found it only in the pomp of paid institutions, and in a help well meant, no doubt, yet carrying little of what was most essential, sympathetic discrimination, and mild, nay even tender care. Within the half-century a new chapter has opened. Faith and love have gone forth into the field. Specimens of womankind, sometimes the very best and highest, have not deemed this quest of souls beneath them. Scrimping of wages, no doubt, there is and was. But the fair wage of today is far higher than it was then, and the unfair wage is assumably not lower. Miserable and crowded dwellings, again, and fever as their result, both then and now. But legislation has in the interval made its attempts in earnest; and if this was with awkward and ungainly hand, private munificence or enterprise is dotting our city areas with worthy dwellings. With all this there has happily grown up not only a vast general extension of benevolent and missionary means, but a great parochial machinery of domestic visitation, charged with comfort and blessing to the needy, and spread over so wide a circle, that what was formerly an exception may now with some confidence be said to be the rule. If insufficiencies have come to be more keenly felt, is that because they are greater, or because there is a bolder and better trained disposition to feel them?

Tennyson was not alone in his questioning: there had been a 'rediscovery' of poverty by the middle classes in the 1880s, a realisation that in spite of the triumphant advance of industry, many had been left behind, workless and in squalor. The 'Bloody Sunday' riot in Trafalgar Square on 13 November 1887 acted as a forceful reminder, though Lady Monkswell viewed it unsympathetically.

The so-called 'unemployed' and a good contingent of roughs had taken possession of the space round Nelson's Column in Trafalgar Square since the middle of October, and had persistently slept there and held meetings assisted by the Socialists and the extreme Radicals.

The 'unemployed' announced that they were going to hold a meeting in Trafalgar Square and 'come in their thousands' on Sunday 13th to protest against the imprisonment of O'Brien, an Irish Member, who had most properly been locked up for seditious language, and also to assert their right of public meeting. Sir Charles Warren (the head of the police) gave notice that they might hold as many meetings as they liked in Hyde Park but they should not meet in Trafalgar Square. Sunday 13th of November arrived, and some Radical and all the Socialist Clubs from all parts of the town set off followed by the whole criminal population and vast numbers of sightseers, who came to see the fun—for Trafalgar Square. Sir Charles Warren was quite ready for them with five thousand policemen, and stopped them in Northumberland Avenue and Parliament Street, and a great fight began, the policemen with fists and occasionally batons, and the crowd with stones, sticks, iron bars, anything they could get. The police were quite able to hold their own but were getting rather exhausted, so Warren ordered up a troop of the Horse Guards, who slowly walked round the Square while the crowd *cheered them*, and afterwards a division of the Foot Guards, who stood along the front of the National Gallery.

70

The riot on Bloody Sunday, 1887, in Trafalgar Square

Charles Booth was a wealthy shipowner who had come to live in London in about 1880. He thought exaggerated a claim made in 1885 that a quarter of the working class lived in poverty, so set about his own investigation. Before long, he found that, as far as the East End of London was concerned, the figure was 35 per cent, and 30 per cent for the rest of the capital. First he describes conditions in two streets either side of Drury Lane:

The houses were about forty in number and few of the two hundred families who lived here [Shelton Street] occupied more than one room. In little rooms no more than 8 feet square, would be found living father, mother, and several children. Some of the rooms would have a recess 6 feet wide for the bed, which in rare instances would be curtained off. If

71

there was no curtain, anyone lying on the bed would perhaps be covered up and hidden, head and all, when a visitor was admitted, or perhaps no shyness would be felt. Most of the people described are Irish Roman Catholics getting a living as market porters, or by selling flowers, fruit, fowls, or vegetables in the streets, but as to not a few it is a mystery how they live. Drunkenness and dirt and bad language prevailed, and violence was common, reaching at times even to murder. Fifteen rooms out of twenty were filthy to the last degree, and the furniture in none of these would be worth 20s., in some cases not 5s. Not a room would be free from vermin, and in many life at night was unbearable. Several occupants have said that in hot weather they don't go to bed, but sit in their clothes in the least infested part of the room. What good is it, they said, to go to bed when you can't get a wink of sleep for bugs and fleas? A visitor in these rooms was fortunate indeed if he carried nothing of the kind away with him. The passage from the street to the back door would be scarcely ever swept, to say nothing of being scrubbed. Most of the doors stood open all night as well as all day, and the passage and stairs gave shelter to many who were altogether homeless. Here the mother could stand with her baby, or sit with it on the stairs, or companions would huddle together in cold weather. The little yard at the back was only sufficient for dustbin and closet and water-tap, serving for six or seven families. The water would be drawn from cisterns which were receptacles for refuse, and perhaps occasionally a dead cat.

Gambling was the amusement of the street. Sentries would be posted, and if the police made a rush the offenders would slip into the open houses and hide until danger was past. Sunday afternoon and evening was the hey-day time for this street. Every doorstep would be crowded by those who sat or stood with pipe and jug of beer, while lads lounged about, and the gutters would find amusement for not a few children with bare feet, their faces and hands besmeared, while the mud oozed through between their toes. Add to this a group of fifteen or twenty young men gambling in the middle of the street and you complete the general picture.

Daddy's Waistcoat –
this was sketched from life in Drury Lane by Phil May

In the first floor front [of No. 6 Parker Street] lived a big Irish woman with two children, and with them a young woman of about twenty-seven years, whose life was that of a fallen woman—in the room all day and out at night. Six years ago this woman, who then lived in Neal Street, was lying helpless in bed suffering from the kick of a disappointed policeman, who was tried and got nine months for the offence.

No. 8 is a lodging-house for women. An underground room, reached by stairs from the entrance passage, serves as the common kitchen and is

POLICE *THE ILLUSTRATED* NEWS
LAW COURTS AND WEEKLY RECORD

No. 1,284.   SATURDAY, SEPTEMBER 22, 1888.   Price One Penny.

"IS HE THE WHITECHAPEL MURDERER?"

READY FOR THE WHITECHAPEL FIEND. WOMEN SECRETLY ARMED.

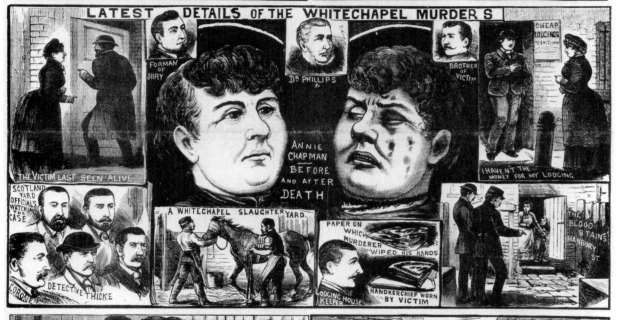

LATEST DETAILS OF THE WHITECHAPEL MURDERS

FOREMAN OF JURY

DR PHILLIPS

BROTHER OF VICTIM

CHEAP LODGINGS

THE VICTIM LAST SEEN ALIVE

ANNIE CHAPMAN BEFORE AND AFTER DEATH

I HAVEN'T THE MONEY FOR MY LODGING

SCOTLAND YARD OFFICIALS WATCHING THE CASE

CORONER   DETECTIVE THICKE

A WHITECHAPEL SLAUGHTER YARD.

PAPER ON WHICH MURDERER WIPED HIS HANDS

LODGING HOUSE KEEPER

HANDKERCHIEF WORN BY VICTIM

THE BLOOD STAINS HANBURY ST

EXCITING SCENE IN BOSTOCK AND WOMBWELL'S MENAGERIE

MORE HORRIBLE MYSTERIES.

The popular Press has a field day with the Jack the Ripper case

about 11 feet by 13 feet. In this room is a large red-hot coke fire, and round about are rough tables and benches. Here at times may be seen about twenty women with matted hair, and face and hands most filthy, whose ragged clothing is stiff with accumulations of beer and dirt, their under-clothing, if they have any at all, swarming with vermin. Many of them are often drunk. These women are thieves, beggars, and prostitutes. If any woman from the country is unfortunate enough to come amongst them she will surely be robbed of all that can be taken from her, and then, un-fit for anything else, may fall to the level of the rest. Bad as this house is here described, it was worse in the days of the famous or infamous Mrs Collins, a gigantic woman profusely bedecked with rings, who grew enormously fat and died weighing nearly 30 stone. She made her money it was said by combining the role of lodging-house keeper with that of procuress.

Within the East End, the Whitechapel area gained a particular notoriety in 1888 thanks to a series of murders of prostitutes there. The butchery practised on the girls by 'Jack the Ripper' and the fact that he was never caught has kept the story alive ever since, and allowed the wildest specula-tion as to who he might have been. Charles Booth describes the area:

This excitement of life which can accept murder as a dramatic incident and drunkenness as the buffoonery of the stage is especially characteris-tic of Whitechapel. And looked at in this way, what a drama it is! Whitechapel is a veritable Tom Tiddler's ground, the Eldorado of the East, a gathering together of poor fortune-seekers; its streets are full of buying and selling, the poor living on the poor. Here, just outside the old City walls, have always lived the Jews, and here they are now in thou-sands, both old-established and newcomers, seeking their livelihood under conditions which seem to suit them, on the middle ground between civilisation and barbarism.

The neighbourhood of old Petticoat Lane on Sunday is one of the wonders of London, a medley of strange sights, strange sounds, and strange smells. Streets crowded so as to be thoroughfares no longer, and lined with a double or treble row of handbarrows, set fast with empty cases, so as to assume the guise of market stalls. Here and there a cart may have been drawn in, but the horse has gone and the tilt is used as a rostrum whence the salemen with stentorian voices cry their wares, vying with each other in introducing to the surrounding crowd their cheap garments, smart braces, sham jewellery, or patent medicines.

Near the Great Eastern Station [Liverpool Street] is the market of the 'fancy'. Here the streets are blocked with those coming to buy, or sell,

Lillie, *a slum child, by Whistler*

pigeons, canaries, rabbits, fowls, parrots, or guinea pigs, and with them or separately all the appurtenances of bird- or pet-keeping. Through this crowd the seller of shellfish pushes his barrow; on the outskirts of it are moveable shooting galleries, and patent Aunt Sallies, while some man standing up in a dog-cart will dispose of racing tips in sealed envelopes to the East End sportsman.

The urgent cries of the seller seem to be accepted on both sides as necessary, though entirely useless. Not infrequently the goods are sold by a sort of Dutch auction—then the prices named are usually double what the seller, and every bystander, knows to be the market price of the street and day, 'Eightpence?' 'Sevenpence?' 'Sixpence?' 'Fivepence?' ——say 'Fourpence?'—well, then, 'Threepence halfpenny?' A bystander, probably a woman, nods imperceptibly; the fish or whatever it is passes from the right hand of the seller·on which it has been raised to view, on to the square of newspaper, resting on his left hand, is bundled

75

up and quick as thought takes its place in the buyer's basket in exchange for the 3½d., which finds its place in the seller's apron or on the board beside the fish—and then begins again the same routine, 'Eightpence?' 'Sevenpence?' 'Sixpence?' etc.

Here Charles Booth describes the mechanics of prostitution:

In every case the women need protection and in nearly every case it is secured. Thus in the brothel, besides the house mistress, who is usually a forcible, middle-aged woman, there is always a man in reserve who can act as 'chucker-out' if required; and a house of accommodation takes care to be equally well provided; while those women who habitually bring strangers to their own private rooms must exercise a good deal of prudence and, excepting as regards women of a rather superior class, do in fact rarely live alone, being usually associated with a man who shares their earnings, and in case of need can take their part. These men are known as 'bullies', and the word may describe equally their position towards the woman or her clients. The relations between prostitute and protector in this unhallowed association have, it would seem, something of the character of a marriage—the tie a lasting one, and the woman often devoted to the man even though very roughly treated. Indeed it is said the rougher the man the more devoted the woman, his roughness, perhaps, making him the better protector. The only utterly exposed class are the low women, who, under cover of darkness, make use of back streets and open spaces, and whose unprotected state gave rise to the horrible tragedies of a few years back.

Charles Booth was assisted in his researches by his wife's cousin Beatrice Potter, later, as Beatrice Webb, a key figure in the Labour movement. She wrote the following account of the arrival of Jewish refugees from eastern Europe:

The crowd gathered in and about the gin-shop overlooking the narrow entrance of the landing-stage are dock loungers of the lowest type and professional 'runners'. These latter individuals, usually of the Hebrew race, are among the most repulsive of East London parasites; boat after boat touches the landing-stage, they push forward, seize hold of the bundles or baskets of the newcomers, offer bogus tickets to those who wish to travel forward to America, promise guidance and free lodging to those who hold in their hands addresses of acquaintances in Whitechapel, or who are absolutely friendless. A little man with an official badge (*Hebrew Ladies' Protective Society*) fights valiantly in their

76

A young flower-girl outside St-Martin-in-the-Fields. Painting by William Logsdail

midst for the conduct of unprotected females, and shouts or whispers to the others to go to the Poor Jews' Temporary Shelter in Leman Street. For a few moments it is a scene of indescribable confusion: cries and counter-cries; the hoarse laughter of the dock loungers at the strange garb and broken accent of the poverty-stricken foreigners; the rough swearing of the boatmen at passengers unable to pay the fee for landing. In another ten minutes eighty of the hundred newcomers are dispersed in the back slums of Whitechapel; in another few days, the majority of these, robbed of the little they possess, are turned out of the 'free lodgings' destitute and friendless.

If we were able to follow the 'greener' into the next scene of his adventures we should find him existing on the charity of a co-religionist or toiling day and night for a small labour-contractor in return for a shake-down, a cup of black coffee, and a hunch of brown bread. This state of dependence, however, does not last. For a time the man works as if he were a slave under the lash, silently, without complaint. But in a few months (in the busy season in a few weeks) the master enters his workshop and the man is not at his place. He has left without warning—silently—as he worked without pay. He has learnt his trade and can sell his skill in the open market at the corner of Commercial Street; or possibly a neighbouring sweater, pressed with work, has offered him better terms. A year hence he has joined a Chevras,* or has become an habitué of a gambling club. And unless he falls a victim to the Jewish passion for gambling, he employs the enforced leisure of the slack season in some form of petty dealing. He is soon in a fair way to become a tiny capitalist—a maker of profit as well as an earner of wage. He has moved out of the back court in which his fellow-countrymen are herded together like animals, and is comfortably installed in a model dwelling; the walls of his parlour are decked with prints of Hebrew worthies, or with portraits of prize-fighters and race-horses; his wife wears jewellery and furs on the Sabbath; for their Sunday dinner they eat poultry. He treats his wife with courtesy and tenderness, and they discuss constantly the future of the children. He is never to be seen at the public-house round the corner; but he enjoys a quiet glass of 'rum and shrub' and a game of cards with a few friends on the Saturday or Sunday evening; and he thinks seriously of season tickets for the People's Palace.† He remembers the starvation fare and the long hours of his first place: he remembers, too, the name and address of the wholesale house served by his first master; and presently he appears at the counter and offers to take the work at a lower

* Half benefit club and half association for religious worship.
† A recently established philanthropic place of uplifting entertainment and study in the East End.

78

Striking match girls

figure, or secures it through a tip to the foreman. But he no longer kisses the hand of Singer's agent and begs with fawning words for another sewing-machine; neither does he flit to other lodgings in the dead of night at the first threat of the broker. In short, he has become a law-abiding and self-respecting citizen of our great metropolis, and feels himself the equal of a Montefiore or a Rothschild.

Annie Besant, journalist, theosophist, and early champion of contraception, campaigned for the London match workers. Here is her 1888 article, which led to a boycott and then to a successful strike.

Bryant and May, now a limited liability company, paid last year a dividend of 23 per cent to its shareholders; two years ago it paid a dividend of 25 per cent, and the original £5 shares were then quoted for sale at £18 7s. 6d. The highest dividend paid has been 38 per cent.

Let us see how the money is made with which these monstrous dividends are paid . . .

The hour for commencing work is half-past six in summer and eight in winter; work concludes at six p.m. Half an hour is allowed for breakfast and an hour for dinner. This long day of work is performed by young girls, who have to stand the whole of the time. A typical case is that of a girl of sixteen, a piece-worker; she earns 4s. a week, and lives with a sister, employed by the same firm, who 'earns good money, as much as 8s. or 9s. per week'. Out of the earnings 2s. is paid for the rent of one room; the child lives on only bread-and-butter and tea, alike for breakfast and dinner, but related with dancing eyes that once a month she went to a meal where 'you get coffee, and bread and butter, and jam, and marmalade, and lots of it' . . . The splendid salary of 4s. is subject to deductions in the shape of fines; if the feet are dirty, or the ground under the bench is left untidy, a fine of 3d. is inflicted; for putting 'burnts'—matches that have caught fire during the work—on the bench 1s. has been forfeited, and one unhappy girl was once fined 2s. 6d. for some unknown crime. If a girl leaves four or five matches on her bench when she goes for a fresh 'frame' she is fined 3d., and in some departments a fine of 3d. is inflicted for talking. If a girl is late she is shut out for 'half the day', that is for the morning six hours, and 5d. is deducted out of her day's 8d. One girl was fined 1s. for letting the web twist around a machine in the endeavour to save her fingers from being cut, and was sharply told to take care of the machine, 'never mind your fingers'. Another, who carried out the instructions and lost a finger thereby, was left unsupported while she was helpless. The wage covers the duty of submitting to an occasional blow from a foreman; one, who appears to be a gentleman of variable temper, 'clouts' them 'when he is mad'.

One department of the work consists in taking matches out of a frame and putting them into boxes; about three frames can be done in an hour, and ½d. is paid for each frame emptied; only one frame is given out at a time, and the girls have to run downstairs and upstairs each time to fetch the frame, thus much increasing their fatigue. One of the delights of the frame work is the accidental firing of the matches: when this happens the worker loses the work, and if the frame is injured she is fined or 'sacked'. Five shillings a week had been earned at this by one girl I talked to.

The 'fillers' get ¾d. a gross for filling boxes; at 'boxing', i.e. wrapping papers round the boxes, they can earn from 4s. 6d. to 5s. a week. A very rapid 'filler' has been known to earn once 'as much as 9s.' in a week, and 6s. a week 'sometimes'. The making of boxes is not done in the factory; for these 2¼d. a gross is paid to people who work in their own homes, and 'find your own paste'. Daywork is a little better paid than piecework, and is done chiefly by married women, who earn as much sometimes as 10s. a week, the piecework falling to the girls. Four women day workers, spoken of with reverent awe, earn—13s. a week.

A very bitter memory survives in the factory. Mr Theodore Bryant, to

show his admiration of Mr Gladstone and the greatness of his own public spirit, bethought him to erect a statue to that eminent statesman. In order that his workgirls might have the privilege of contributing, he stopped 1s. each out of their wages, and further deprived them of half-a-day's work by closing the factory, 'giving them a holiday'. ('We don't want no holidays,' said one of the girls pathetically, for—needless to say—the poorer employees of such a firm lose their wages when a holiday is 'given'.) So furious were the girls at this cruel plundering, that many went to the unveiling of the statue with stones and bricks in their pockets, and I was conscious of a wish that some of those bricks had made an impression on Mr Bryant's conscience. Later on they surrounded the statue—'we paid for it' they cried savagely—shouting and yelling, and a gruesome story is told that some cut their arms and let their blood trickle on the marble paid for, in very truth, by their blood . . .

Such is a bald account of one form of white slavery as it exists in London. With chattel slaves Mr Bryant could not have made his huge fortune, for he could not have fed, clothed, and housed them for 4s. a week each, and they would have had a definite money value which would have served as a protection. But who cares for the fate of these white wage slaves? Born in slums, driven to work while still children, undersized because underfed, oppressed because helpless, flung aside as soon as worked out, who cares if they die or go on the streets, provided only that the Bryant and May shareholders get their 23 per cent, and Mr Theodore Bryant can erect statues and buy parks? Oh if we had but a people's Dante, to make a special circle in the Inferno for those who live on this misery, and suck wealth out of the starvation of helpless girls.

Failing a poet to hold up their conduct to the execration of posterity, enshrined in deathless verse, let us strive to touch their consciences, i.e. their pockets, and let us at least avoid being 'partakers of their sins', by abstaining from using their commodities.

One of the publishing sensations of 1896 was a novel called A Child of the Jago, *about life in one of the worst recesses of the East End, where abject poverty shaded into hereditary criminality. Its author, the journalist Arthur Morrison, came from a working-class background in Poplar, and did additional research in the Old Nichol, part of Shoreditch, in 1895, before he began the book. In the first extract he describes 'the major industry of the Jago'. Then comes the high point of the book: the fight between Billy Leary and Josh Perrott.*

A woman, gripping a shawl about her shoulders, came furtively along from the posts, with a man walking in her tracks—a little unsteadily. He was not of the Jago, but a decent young workman, by his dress. The sight took Kiddo Cook's idle eye, and when the couple had passed, he said meditatively: 'There's Billy Leary in luck ag'in: 'is missis do pick 'em up, s'elp me. I'd carry the cosh meself if I'd a woman like 'er.'

Cosh-carrying was near to being the major industry of the Jago. The cosh was a foot length of iron rod, with a knob at one end, and a hook (or a ring) at the other. The craftsman, carrying it in his coat sleeve, waited about dark staircase corners till his wife (married or not) brought in a well-drunken stranger: when, with a sudden blow behind the head, the stranger was happily coshed, and whatever was found on him as he lay insensible was the profit on the transaction. In the hands of capable practitioners this industry yielded a comfortable subsistence for no great exertion. Most, of course, depended on the woman: whose duty it was to keep the other artist going in subjects. There were legends of surprising ingatherings achieved by wives of especial diligence: one of a woman who had brought to the cosh some six-and-twenty on a night of public rejoicing. This was, however, a story years old, and may have been no more than an exemplary fiction, designed, like a Sunday School book, to convey a counsel of perfection to the dutiful matrons of the Old Jago.

Minding a child for a younger woman who has found work

The man and woman vanished in a doorway near the Jago Row end, where, for some reason, dossers were fewer than about the portal of Jago Court. There conversation flagged, and a broken snore was heard. It was a quiet night, as quietness was counted in the Jago; for it was too hot for most to fight in that stifling air—too hot to do more than turn on the stones and swear. Still the last hoarse yelps of a combat of women came intermittently from Half Jago Street in the further confines.

In a little while something large and dark was pushed forth from the door-opening near Jago Row which Billy Leary's spouse had entered. The thing rolled over, and lay tumbled on the pavement, for a time unnoted. It might have been yet another would-be sleeper, but for its stillness. Just such a thing it seemed, belike, to two that lifted their heads and peered from a few yards off, till they rose on hands and knees and crept to where it lay: Jago rats both. A man it was; with a thick smear across his face, and about his head the source of the dark trickle that sought the gutter deviously over the broken flags. The drab stuff of his pockets peeped out here and there in a crumpled bunch, and his waist-coat gaped where the watch-guard had been. Clearly, here was an uncommonly remunerative cosh—a cosh so good that the boots had been neglected, and remained on the man's feet. These the kneeling two unlaced deftly, and, rising, prize in hand, vanished in the deeper shadow of Jago Row.

Presently down came the High Mobsmen, swaggering in check suits and billycocks, gold chains and lumpy rings: stared at, envied, and here and there pointed out by name or exploit. 'Him as done the sparks in from Regent Street for nine centuries o' quids'; 'Him as done five stretch for a snide bank bill an' they never found the 'oof'; 'Him as maced the bookies in France an' shot the nark in the boat'; and so forth. And the High Mob being come, the fight was due.

Josh Perrott had been strictly sober for a full week. And the family had lived better, for he had brought meat home each day. Now he sat indifferently at the window of his room, and looked out at the crowd in Jago Court till such time as he might be wanted. He had not been out of the room that morning: he was saving his energy for Billy Leary.

Presently Jerry Gullen and Kiddo Cook came, as seconds, to take Josh out. Josh dragged off his spotted coat and waistcoat and flung them on the bed, and then was helped out of his ill-mended blue shirt. He gave a hitch to his trousers-band, tightened his belt, and was ready.

'Ta-ta, ol' gal,' he said to his wife, with a grin; 'back agin soon.'

'With a bob or two for ye,' added Kiddo Cook, grinning likewise.

Hannah Perrott sat pale and wistful, with the baby Looey on her knees.

'Aincher goin' to look, mother?' Dicky Perrott asked. 'Wontcher 'old up Looey?'

But his mother would not look. As for Looey, she looked at nothing. She had been taken to the dispensary once again, and now lay drowsy and dull, with little more movement than a general shudder and a twitching of the face at long intervals. The little face itself was thinner and older than ever: horribly fleabitten still, but bloodlessly pale. Mrs Perrott had begun to think Looey was ailing for something; thought it might be measles or whooping-cough coming, and complained that children were a continual worry.

Now there was an irregular space of bare cobble stones and house refuse, five or six yards across, in the middle of Jago Court, and all round it the shouting crowd was packed tight, those at the back standing on sills and hanging to fences. Every window was a clump of heads, and

84

A MISUNDERSTANDING.

women yelled savagely or cheerily down and across. The two groups were merged in the press at each side of the space, Billy Leary and Josh Perrott in front of each, with his seconds.

'Naa then, any more 'fore they begin?' bawled a High Mobsman, turning about among his fellows. 'Three to one on the big 'un—three to one! 'Ere I'll give fours—four to one on Leary! Fourer one! Fourer one!'

But they shook their heads; they would wait a little. Leary and Perrott stepped out. The last of the tossers stuffed away his coppers, and sought for a hold on the fence.

'They're a-sparrin', mother!' cried Dicky, pale and staring, elbows and legs a-work, till he was like to pitch out of the window. From his mother there but jerked a whimpering sob, which he did not hear.

The sparring was not long. There was little of subtlety in the milling of the Jago: mostly no more than a rough application of the main hits and guards, with much rushing and ruffianing. What there was of condition in the two men was Josh's: smaller and shorter, he had a certain hard brownness of hide that Leary, in his heavy opulence of flesh, lacked; and there was a horny quality in his face and hands that reminded the company of his boast of invulnerability to anything milder than steel. Also his breadth of chest was great. Nevertheless all odds seemed against him, by reason of Billy Leary's size, reach, and fighting record.

Following pages: The magnificent skyline of St Pancras
Station from the Pentonville Road, by John O'Connor

The men rushed together, and Josh was forced back by weight. Leary's great fists, left and right, shot into his face with smacking reports, but left no mark on the leathery skin, and Josh, fighting for the body, drove his knuckles into the other's ribs with a force that jerked a thick grunt from Billy's lips at each blow.

There was a roar of shouts. 'Go it, father! Fa—ther! Fa—ther!' Dicky screamed from the window, till his voice broke in his throat and he coughed himself livid. The men were at holds, and swaying this way and that over the uneven stones. Blood ran copiously from Billy Leary's nose over his mouth and chin, and, as they turned, Dicky saw his father spit away a tooth over Leary's shoulder. They clipped and hauled to and fro, each striving to break the other's foothold. Then Perrott stumbled at a hole, lost his feet, and went down, with Leary on top.

Cheers and yells rent the air, as each man was taken to his own side by his seconds. Dicky let go the sill and turned to his mother, wild of eye, breathless with broken chatter.

'Father 'it 'im on the nose, mother, like that—'is ribs is goin' black where father pasted 'em—'e was out o' breath fust—there's blood all over 'is face, mother—father would 'a' chucked 'im over if 'e'adn't tumbled in a 'ole—father 'it 'im twice on the jore—'e—Oh!'

Dicky was back again on the sill, kicking and shouting, for time was called, and the two men rushed again into a tangled knot. But the close strife was short. Josh had but closed to spoil his man's wind, and, leaving his head to take care of itself, stayed till he had driven left and right on the mark, and then got back. Leary came after him, gasping and blowing already, and Josh feinted a lead and avoided, bringing Leary round on his heel and off again in chase. Once more Josh met him, drove at his ribs, and got away out of reach. Leary's wind was going fast, and his partisans howled savagely at Josh—perceiving his tactics—taunting him with running away, daring him to stand and fight. 'I'll take that four to one,' called a High Mobsman to him who had offered the odds in the beginning. 'I'll stand a quid on Perrott!'

'Not with me you won't,' the other answered. 'Evens, if you like.'

'Right. Done at evens. A quid.'

Perrott, stung at length by the shouts from Leary's corner, turned on Billy and met him at full dash. He was himself puffing by this time, though much less than his adversary, and, at the cost of a heavy blow (which he took on his forehead), he visited Billy's ribs once more.

Both men were grunting and gasping now, and the sound of blows was as of the confused beating of carpets. Dicky, who had been afflicted to heartburst by his father's dodging and running, which he mistook for simple flight, now broke into excited speech once more:

'Father's 'it 'im on the jore ag'in—'is eye's a-bungin' up—*Go it, father, bash 'i-i-i-m*! Father's landin' 'im—'e——'

Hannah Perrott crept to the window and looked. She saw the foul Jago mob, swaying and bellowing about the shifting edge of an open patch, in the midst whereof her husband and Billy Leary, bruised, bloody and gasping, fought and battered infuriately; and she crept back to the bed and bent her face on Looey's unclean little frock; till a fit of tense shuddering took the child, and the mother looked up again.

Without, the round ended. For a full minute the men took and gave knock for knock, and then Leary, wincing from another body-blow, swung his right desperately on Perrott's ear, and knocked him over.

But Josh is soon up and in the next round he eventually overcomes the heavier man and receives a princely five pounds in winnings. His wife is hauled off to celebrate with him and baby Looey, forgotten, dies.

What of the rural poor? L. E. Jones, son of the squire of Cranmer Hall in Norfolk, remembered them in the first volume of his autobiography, A Victorian Boyhood.

That this was a world of pre-ordained classes, we never doubted. We felt no sense of patronage when, on Christmas Eve, the cottagers on the estate crowded into the decorated Servants' Hall, each man bringing with him a capacious red-and-white spotted handkerchief. This he unrolled upon a long trestle table, and we children set upon each handkerchief, with our bare hands, a chunk of raw and bleeding beef, and a packet of raisins done up in thick purple paper with a piece of holly stuck into it. My father came in and wished them all a Merry Christmas, and they wished him the same, not forgetting the young ladies and gentlemen. We were not class-conscious, because class was something that was there, like the rest of the phenomenal world; moreover, they were all our respected friends, who simply happened to be 'the poor', and consequently could not expect to dine, like ourselves, off turkey and plumpudding. When we visited them in their homes, we were prone to envy them for their warmth and cosiness, the shell-boxes, the grandfather clocks, the china dogs upon the mantelpiece, rather than to compare their cramped dwellings unfavourably with our own.

Nobody told us that the widow Grimmer was bringing up two boys on 5s. a week from the parish, and lighting in her grate, from time to time, a piece of brown paper, in order that she and the children might warm their hands, for three or four fleeting seconds, when the paper flamed and roared in the draught of the crooked chimney. Did my father, the

Ploughing, by Sir George Clausen

kindest of men, know this? He was paying his farm-labourers, married men with families, 14s. a week. But they were lucky, for they got free milk and butter from Mrs Olley's dairy. Did my father know that young Willy Woodhouse, aged seventeen, who worked in the carpenters' shop, walked seven miles in the morning, with his tool-bag on his back, to repair the barn at Kettlestone, and seven miles home again at night? Old John Basham, the head-carpenter, drove there in his cart, to keep an eye on the work. My father swore by old John Basham, and selected, for old John's tombstone, after much thought, the text: 'The path of the just is as a shining light, that shineth more and more unto the perfect day.' But if John Basham was about to return from Kettlestone half an hour before knocking-off time, not once did it occur to his just mind to wait and give his workmen, or at worst their heavy tools, a lift home in his pony-cart. He rode the path of the just behind his pony, and Sam and young Willy trudged again the seven miles of dusty lanes. Estate carpenters, in those days, received class as something 'given', as we did, together with most of the men on the place. Hard work, thoroughness, and pride in the job were the marks of those men; their endurance, patience, and asceticism were taken for granted by themselves as much as by their employer.

I have learnt since, from a survivor of this generation still living, that their lives were not enviable ones, and that their virtue did not bring its own reward. They suffered. I do not remember hearing one word spoken, by my parents or by the farm labourers whom we so often 'hindered

90

more than we helped' in hay and harvest field, that hinted at the stubborn nineteenth-century contention, not least sharp in East Anglia, over agricultural wages. What did reach us was a talk of low rents, and of rents remitted, and of the losses of the Home Farm. One by one, the laundry was closed, the footman left, and after him the groom; my father's riding-horse was sold. We were partly aware, in short, of the economic conditions of the Nineties as they touched ourselves; we knew nothing of the cottager's, nothing of the tenant-farmer's distresses.

The world of the poor, whether urban or rural, did not impinge on Queen Victoria. E. F. Benson remarked that

her lack of imagination led her into errors from which her common sense could not save her. She knew nothing whatever of the working classes, of the barbarous beggary, of the poverty and suffering and squalor in which they lived, and when some inarticulate protest from below seethed up into hoarse murmurings and mutterings, she heard in them nothing but the threats of rioters and revolutionaries who uttered menaces against all which made for stability and ordered government. She was a firm believer in classes, but she knew of only three: first came monarchy, then came the upper and landed class which directly buttressed the throne, thirdly there was the great middle class which she saw was becoming the governing power. Below it there came no doubt a very large quantity of dim human beings, but of these she neither saw nor heard anything to any purpose. There were, of course, crofters round about Balmoral, and she took much interest in their affairs, especially their funerals and their marriages, and she records the visits she made in order to see how the 'poor people' lived. But her knowledge of any class below the middle class was limited to such as these.

The Queen did not like to be photographed smiling because of her very small teeth, but here she is captured with Princess Beatrice (standing) and Princess Victoria, seated with her daughter Alice, mother of the present Duke of Edinburgh, on her knee

The Queen's Household

The 'elegant libels' of Lytton Strachey's book Eminent Victorians *were behind him when he came to write his biography of the Queen in 1921, and his tone can only be called affectionate as he describes the routines of her old age. He is followed by Emily Lytton's mother describing an afternoon drive with the Queen at Balmoral in October 1895. During the course of it they make a call on a crofter. As E. F. Benson said in the concluding extract of the previous chapter, crofters were the only members of the lower orders with whom the Queen was at all familiar.*

Lytton Strachey

Her life passed in an extraordinary exactitude. Every moment of her day was mapped out beforehand; the succession of her engagements was immutably fixed. She demanded from those who surrounded her a rigid precision in details, and she was preternaturally quick in detecting the slightest deviation from the rules which she had laid down. Such was the irresistible potency of her personality, that anything but the most implicit obedience to her wishes was felt to be impossible. [As long as she got this] her smile, once so rare a visitant to those saddened features, flitted over them with an easy alacrity; the blue eyes beamed; the whole face, starting suddenly from its pendulous expressionlessness, brightened and softened and cast over those who watched it an unforgettable charm. For in her last years there was a fascination in Victoria's amiability which had been lacking even from the vivid impulse of her youth. Over all who approached her—or very nearly all—she threw a peculiar spell. Her grandchildren adored her; her ladies waited upon her with a reverential love. The honour of serving her obliterated a thousand inconveniences —the monotony of a court existence, the fatigue of standing, the necessity for a superhuman attentiveness to the minutiae of time and space. As one did one's wonderful duty one could forget that one's legs were aching from the infinitude of the passages at Windsor, or that one's bare arms were turning blue in the Balmoral cold.

I had been told I was to drive with the Queen and Princess Christian at four, so I went at once to dress warm as the order (from the Scotch piper who sings his words and is very difficult to understand) included tea at some lodge, and I knew we should be home late.

The process of getting Her Majesty into the carriage is intricate, with a green baize plank slanting up from the door-step. Then the Indian servant supports the Queen the most, and so gently, and without any fear or nervousness, then there were cloaks, shawls, and frills offered by different hands. Princess Christian seemed terribly afraid of taking too much room, and sat right forward and I opposite. Then the many rugs were brought in turn. At last the two outriders on greys and the four beautifully driven-in-hand greys started off. I felt rather inclined to giggle but not at all alarmed.

We stopped at a cottage and the Queen gave a woman a dress so kindly and the small talk never stopped and when the Queen dozed at times the Princess and I went on talking. The tea at the head keeper's, Donald Stewart, was very nice and only Mustafa waited on us, so quickly and well. The scones, Scotch pancakes and jam were all extra perfect, made by Stewart, and we all ate much more than we ought. The drive back was quite short.

Marie Mallet, who was first a maid-of-honour and then, after her marriage in 1891, a lady-in-waiting, recalls the royal round, and then gives some vignettes of life in the Highlands, at Balmoral.

The dates of the rota at Windsor, Osborne and Balmoral seldom varied and the Queen's trip abroad, to which she looked forward with immense delight, was invariably timed to include Easter and to last exactly six weeks. Visits to Balmoral took place from about the end of April until after Ascot Week. I was always chosen to accompany Her Majesty in the spring and also had to go there for the last three or four weeks in the autumn when the cold was intense and the days short and gloomy. Snow was not unusual in May and I can safely say I never remember a warm congenial day in the Highlands during the many months I spent there.

A certain monotony ruled our days wherever we were. Breakfast half-past nine, lunch at two, tea half-past five, dinner half-past eight. The Queen's dinner was supposed to be at a quarter to nine but it was often quarter past nine before she sat down to her simple meal of soup, fish, cold sirloin of beef, sweet and dessert. Her favourite fruits were oranges and pears and monster indigestible apples which would have daunted

most people half her age but she enjoyed them, sometimes sharing a
mammoth specimen with Princess Beatrice, but more often coping with
it alone. Oranges were treated in a very convenient manner; a hole cut in
the top and the juice scooped out with a spoon. The Queen's dinner was
timed to last exactly half an hour. The service was so rapid that a slow
eater such as myself or Mr Gladstone never had time to finish even a
most moderate helping. Pecking like a bird I usually managed to satisfy
my hunger but could not enjoy the excellent fare handed so expedi-
tiously. Campbell, the Queen's piper in kilt, etc. dispensed the claret or
sherry, champagne was poured out by the butlers, while the Indian servants handed the sweets in a cat-like manner, never forgetting which particular kind of chocolate or biscuit each guest preferred, so twisting the
dish in order that it could be taken with apparent ease.

[1890] First painting for the Princess [Beatrice?] (she begins things and
gets me to finish them off, but do not repeat this); then trotting for an
hour beside the Queen, who to my intense astonishment ascended a
huge ladder in order to mount a horse twenty-six years old, which

pranced along quite gaily, only conceive what energy at seventy-one! Then at three p.m. more painting and half-past four a drive of at least twenty-four miles with the Queen. We were not in till eight, and the wind was so cold my face turned first blue and then crimson and by dinner-time I looked as if I had been drinking hard for a week.

[1895] At eleven p.m. the Queen leaves the drawing-room and I wait in my bedroom till I am summoned at twenty or a quarter to twelve and go to the Queen in her sitting-room where I talk and read and take orders till about half-past twelve, then 'good-night' and I fly to my bed and hot-water bottle! I do not keep up my maid. This routine never varies by a hair's breadth, as soon a revolution as to drive in the morning and walk after lunch, and boiled beef on Thursday and '*mehlspeise mit ananas*' [pudding with pineapple] on Friday recur with unfailing regularity.

The King of Portugal arrived this morning looking fat and pink just like a prize pig. After a heavy lunch the 'Portugeese' as we call them were taken for a chilly drive in our wagonette which they insisted on calling a 'charabanc', and then scaled a neighbouring hill carrying torches with all of Her Majesty's Highland retainers; a huge bonfire was lighted at the top, whisky dispensed with a generous hand, and then followed reels outside the front door beautifully danced by some of the pipers of the Black Watch. I have seldom seen anything more graceful than the way one man danced the most intricate steps waving his flaming torch, now high, now low and hooting all the time.

[1896] I have been walking with the Queen this morning and we went to the church to wreathe the tombs of various Browns; HM got out of her chair and laid a bunch of fresh flowers on John Brown's grave with her own hands. The Prince Consort and the Highland tenants share this unique honour, it is really very curious, but do not mention the curious fact.

Lord Rosebery, who succeeded Gladstone as Prime Minister in 1894, said that he thought the drawing-room at Osborne, in the Isle of Wight, the ugliest in the world, until he saw the one at Balmoral. In a similar vein another Prime Minister, Arthur Balfour, said Osborne 'intends to be Italian but only succeeds in being early Victorian'. Marie Mallet underwent as many trials there as at Balmoral:

[1888] I have been playing lawn tennis this morning with Princess Alex [Princess of Wales] and her lady-in-waiting; they can neither of them get

a ball over the net so the game was not exhilarating, and the sun poured down on my head till I felt quite silly; the German Baron causes me some amusement, his English is extremely limited and peculiar, but he insists upon speaking nothing else, and last night discoursed upon the merits of cows without 'corns', I suppose he meant 'horns'. He also talks of 'tennis robes' and evidently thinks me very vulgar for liking gooseberries.

A watercolour of Balmoral, by William Simpson

Last evening I was summoned to warble duets with Prince Henry,* fearfully difficult selections from Gounod's operas, which *he* knew *perfectly well* and which I was expected to sing at sight. I enacted the role of Juliet, Mireille, and I do not know what else while he shouted violent sentiments such as *'ange adorable!'* at me and at one moment it was so comic that I nearly laughed outright; he has a good voice but cannot manage it and sings with very little expression. Princess Beatrice accompanied us and smiled benignly.

E. F. Benson describes a similar ordeal which Alick Yorke (p. 62), groom-in-waiting and uncle to Marie Mallet, had to endure.

Once, when quite an old woman, the Queen suddenly made the portentous announcement to Alick Yorke, who was in waiting, that after lunch

* of Battenberg. Husband of Princess Beatrice.

A watercolour of
Osborne, by William
Leitch

he and she would sing duets. Someone sat down at the piano to play the
accompaniment, and the Queen propped up on the table between the
two vocalists, a copy of Gilbert and Sullivan's opera *Patience*, and found
the place. She said, 'Now, Mr Yorke, you begin,' and Mr Yorke obediently sang to the Queen, 'Prithee, pretty maiden, will you marry me?' He
got through his verse fairly well, and then the Queen in a very clear soft
voice sang, 'Gentle sir, although to marry I'm inclined'. She was much
pleased with herself, and stopped in the middle of her verse to say, 'You
know, Mr Yorke, I was taught singing by Mendelssohn.'

*A piece of modern music was once played to the Queen. 'What is that?' she
asked. 'It's a drinking song, ma'am, by Rubinstein.' 'Nonsense', said the
Queen; 'no such thing! why, you could not drink a cup of tea to that!'*

*The Queen went abroad regularly to France or Italy. Lord Ronald Gower
encountered her at Aix-les-Bains in April 1890.*

I luckily remembered this day being St Beaconsfield's or Primrose Day.*
I bought a nosegay of that flower at the kiosk, which I took to the villa,
and asked Sir Henry Ponsonby to present it to the Queen. There I was
told Her Majesty had invited me to go and see the review on the Cham-

* Lord Beaconsfield's favourite flower, worn in memory of him.

98

béry Road at eleven; accordingly I was at the villa entrance at that time. The Queen told me she was glad to have been so pleasantly reminded of the day by the primroses. 'I had', the Queen added, 'for the moment forgotten that this was the day.' Then Her Majesty got into her carriage drawn by the grey horses. Sir Henry and I followed the household; Prince Henry of Battenberg on horseback with three French officers. We drove some five miles; as our little procession of carriages and horsemen passed through the countryside the peasants turned out of their villages, all agape — especially at the four turbaned Indians. At a cross road, some four miles out of Chambéry and five from Aix, we stopped, and two regiments of the Chasseurs Alpins came briskly marching up the road, with brass bands. The men wore a dark blue uniform, with blue facings, with broad blue waist-belts, with thick walking-sticks stuck behind them. Behind followed a mule train, some eighty big strong animals, bearing provision and ammunition. After the regiments had marched past, they were drawn up on the right of the road, and the Queen drove slowly down the line, while the band played the National Anthem. A picturesque sight and an interesting one, made the more so by the fact of its being the only time since the [Second] Empire that the Queen has reviewed a portion of the French army.

The following year the Queen was further south at Grasse, where her household had to indulge her obsession with 'worms and epitaphs'. Marie Mallet:

The poor housemaid has just breathed her last, it is all very sad and there is a gloom over us all. The Queen went to see her last night and again this afternoon about an hour before she died.

[Later] It is very curious to see how the Queen takes the keenest interest in death and all its horrors, our whole talk has been of coffins and winding sheets. We had a sort of funeral service last night in the dining-room, the coffin in our midst not even screwed down, everyone in evening dress, the servants sobbing; it was too dreadful and got upon my nerves to such an extent that I never slept all night. The Queen was very grieved and placed a wreath on the coffin rather tremblingly; and then the body was removed to the little English church close by and this afternoon we had to visit it again with the Queen. The final funeral is tomorrow and after that we may hope for a little peace.

[Three days later] Today being bitterly cold the Queen elected to drive to Cannes cemetery and visit the tombs of various friends. We started soon after half-past three and were not home till ten to seven! The gentlemen went in a separate carriage full to overflowing with wreaths for the favoured tombs; when we arrived we formed a doleful little procession headed by a blowsy woman, the wife of the Guardian, and slowly proceeded from grave to grave.

For the flavour of Court life at Windsor, Lady Monkswell's diary is a good source. Her husband, holding a junior post in Gladstone's last Government, was 'in waiting' there for the first time in 1893.

17 May—Bob met me at Windsor station and walked me up over the Castle green and through what was originally, I suppose, the drawbridge. The policeman at the gate saluted him most respectfully, indeed he seems to spend a good part of his time in touching his hat. We were admitted at a sort of private door by a very gorgeous footman in red livery, and went a little way down a corridor and there was his room, no. 540. A nice big high room, looking out on to the terrace. Just over the balustrade of the terrace you could see the tops of the tall trees, beeches, ashes, etc. with the rooks sitting in them, the only sounds were the tramp of the sentinel and the songs of the birds. The room was very large and comfortable, full of large easy chairs, a big sofa and a big tent bed covered with an old-fashioned expensive red poplin stuff and a big table with writing things on which was laid a big tea, which we partook of entirely at Her Gracious Majesty's expense. The cups and plates white with a fine and pretty pattern of lilac and gold, with VR and the crown in the centre. Very good tea, splendid cream and butter, the latter stamped VR with the Imperial Crown, rolls, cakes, apples and grapes, and cold chicken for the boys. Presently in came Robert and Gerard [their sons at Eton nearby] so there we were all together as jolly as possible. The boys were extremely amused at hearing that Bob had that morning ordered out a carriage and pair and postilions, and had gloriously driven some twelve or fourteen miles all about Windsor Park.

I remained *perdu* in the room as I did not want to tumble into the arms of any of the maids-of-honour, and Bob took first one boy and then the other to see the library, theatre, corridors, etc. This suited me exactly, and I had indeed a most happy evening. About quarter past eight, when it was time for Bob to be getting into his evening clothes, we bade him farewell, and the boys escorted me back to the station.

18 May—This day must be for ever remembered as the day when Bob dined with the Queen and had a little conversation with her afterwards. He had been told that he would have to be on duty at half-past three, his duty being to open the door of the Queen's little study where she was going to receive first Lord Rosebery (the Minister for Foreign Affairs), and then an envoy from Serbia. About half-past two, a footman came fly-

ing into the room saying 'My lords, my lords, Her Majesty is waiting.' Hearing this appalling news Lord Rosebery and he—Lord R. weighing at least 15 stone—set off to run as hard as they could go, and arrived at the door of the Queen's study (some 60 or 70 yards or so) very red and flustered. So, without waiting for further instructions as to whether he was to knock loud or low and what he was to do if he could not hear the Queen say 'come in', he *knocked*, and at once heard a very clear voice say 'come in'. He opened the door and found himself in a very little room and about 1½ yards from Her Gracious Majesty. She smiled at him most benignly but of course merely said '(fetch) Lord Rosebery'. He shut the door again very gently. By this time Lord Rosebery had recovered his breath so Bob opened the door and said 'Lord Rosebery' who walked in, and Bob shut the door behind him.

He got notice about seven that he was to dine with the Queen at nine o'clock. The dinner was served on some silver plate, some gold and some china. Bob enjoyed his dinner very much, and got on extremely well with Princess Leiningen. She is a clever, good-looking woman of sixty, and speaks English as well as I do. (After immense research we have discovered that she is the daughter-in-law of one of the Duchess of

Kent's sons by her first marriage, she is therefore the Queen's half-niece-in-law.)* The Queen, I am thankful to learn, has no German accent at all. She ate chiefly vegetables and drank a little wine; she ate some sweets, and laughed and talked pleasantly. Bob distinctly saw her asking the Princess Leiningen what sort of a fellow *he* was, and thought very likely she would speak to him after dinner. And this indeed happened. Bob *had* kissed the Queen's hand at the Drawing Room we went to in March, but the Queen had evidently forgotten this, so, after dinner, she came towards him and said 'I forgot you had not kissed my hands, Lord Monkswell,' and he was very glad to go down on one knee and kiss her hand again. This ceremony over (he did it very nicely Lord Carrington told him afterwards) he backed away a little with his usual modesty, but as *she* advanced he understood she was going to say something to him. She talked to him for three or four minutes about things in general, the Imperial Institute, the Royal Academy and so forth. I have no doubt he unconsciously put his head on one side and looked as if he liked it. They stood about in this corridor until about a quarter to eleven, and then the Queen retired.

At the March 1893 Drawing Room referred to above, Lady Monkswell had been 'determined I would have a good look at the little old Queen, and that I accomplished. She looks very old and is incredibly thick and short. But what an expression the little old lady has!' In 1894 Augustus Hare reported 'Lady Salisbury said that her masseuse went constantly to the Queen. She told Lady S. that what appeared to be lameness in the Queen was merely that her feet were too small to support the weight of her body. Her hands are those of a little child.' At the end of that year, Lady Monkswell confirmed that 'she requires help to move about; a Hindu in a turban and white trousers supports her on one side, and she uses a stick. She also has to wear very strong glasses, but she seems to be up to everything, and knows all that is going on.'

In fact the Hindu was in all probability a Muslim, one of several that the Queen took to having about her person. She was proud that she had more Muslim subjects than the Sultan of Turkey and besides, as Sir Henry Ponsonby's son Arthur put it, 'their attendance in their picturesque costumes gave a certain reminder that she was Empress of India.' The first two, who came over in June 1887, Abdul Karim and Mahomet Buksh, began by acting as khitmutgars *(waiters). By September the Queen was reporting to Sir Henry that 'she cannot say what a comfort she finds her Indian servants. Abdul is most handy in helping when she signs by drying the signatures. He learns with extraordinary assiduity . . .' By February*

---

* A mistake by Lady Monkswell. She should have written half-cousin-in-law.

102

The Munshi, painted
for the Queen by
Rudolph Swoboda.
She later copied this
portrait herself

1888 she was learning Hindustani from him: 'Young Abdul is a very strict master and a perfect gentleman . . . Abdul will no longer wait at meals which is what he feels a good deal.' All photographs of him so employed were soon ordered to be destroyed. In 1889 he was made the Queen's Munshi (teacher), the equivalent of her official Indian secretary, and she expected him to join her household 'in the billiard-room and sometimes at meals', much to their disgust. In that year his brother-in-law stole one of her brooches, but when presented with conclusive evidence, she became furious and shouted 'That is what you English call justice.'

At the Highland Games at Braemar in 1890 the Munshi stood, on the Queen's instructions, among her gentlemen. Sir Henry reported, 'The Duke of Connaught [one of the Queen's sons] was angry and spoke to me about it. I replied that if it was wrong, as I did not understand Indian etiquette and HRH did, would it not be better for him to mention it to the Queen. This entirely shut him up.' In 1894 Frederick Ponsonby, another of

Sir Henry's sons then out in India, was asked by the Queen to visit the Munshi's father in Agra. He did so and discovered that, far from being a surgeon-general as the Munshi claimed, he was merely the apothecary at the city gaol. When Frederick came home and reported this to the Queen, he was not asked to dine for a year, although he was by then holding a Court post. In 1895 the Munshi was made a Companion of the Order of the Indian Empire (CIE) by the Queen, in spite of his friendship with one Raffiudin Ahmed, known to be involved in the subversive Muslim Patriotic League back in India. However, the Queen was requested to stop showing the Munshi confidential Indian despatches because of this connection. In that year Lord Wolseley was summoned to Balmoral to kiss the Queen's hand on his appointment as Field Marshal and Commander-in-Chief:

I was very much amused this afternoon, when out for a walk with Colonel Bigge, to see a closed landau pass. In fact, we had to leave the drive and stand in the snow to let it go by. The windows were open, so I asked who was the 'babu' [Bengali clerk] sort of fellow I saw within it with a large turban. 'Oh, that is the Queen's moonshee and his wife and mother,' I was told. 'They go out in the carriage every day.' One must have been in India to realise the position of the man who is thus provided with a carriage, while the Field Marshal, at the head of the Queen's Army, drives in a fly.

The royal household were no doubt well endowed with the racial prejudices of their time, but the Munshi sounds to have been arrogant, dishonest and manipulative. Throughout her life the Queen seemed to enjoy subjecting herself to masterful men — Lord Melbourne, Prince Albert, John Brown — and the Munshi was merely the last of these. He bullied and shouted at her to get his way; she knew she indulged him and when confronted with his misdemeanours by her courtiers, her only way out was to resort to tantrums. When one of her ladies-in-waiting, Harriet Phipps, told her she must choose between him and her household, the Queen swept every item from her desk onto the floor. Only Sir James Reid, her doctor, could, on occasion, make her be honest: 'In the evening the Queen quite broke down to me, and admitted she had played the fool about the Munshi.' But he was himself made ill by the sixteen-page diatribes she sent him on the subject. Lord Salisbury, as reported by Sir James, made the most perceptive comment. 'He believes she really likes the emotional excitement, as being the only form of excitement she can have.' At least her Hindustani lessons eventually paid off, when she was able to address a few words in it to her Indian troops at her Diamond Jubilee.

The Queen's Family

The Queen had nine children of her own and the list of her grandchildren and then great-grandchildren inexorably lengthened through these decades. Only a few of them can be touched on here—first her eldest son, the Prince of Wales. E. F. Benson displays him in the most flattering light.

She kept in her own hands every atom of the more solid functions of the Crown, and instead of consulting her singularly intelligent son, and committing to him those diplomacies and administrations which he, vividly in touch with the times, was so competent to conduct, and which he so sagaciously conducted as soon as he had the chance of doing so, she withheld from him everything of the kind. She refused to let him be Governor-General of Canada or Viceroy of Ireland, and to open a few docks and bazaars and lay a few foundation-stones was not employment for a mentally energetic man, now in the very prime of life, who would have been of inestimable service in Imperial concerns; she even saw in his visit to Ireland reasons for regret that it coincided with the Punchestown races. It was therefore not only natural but laudable that, denied the work to which he longed to devote himself, he used his energies in enjoying himself, for which also he had a very enviable aptitude.

To him more than to anyone was due the break-up of the mid-Victorian social tradition of frozen pompous dignity, and all its repressions and reticences. He toppled over that futile forbidding old idol, he broke down the staid hedges that surrounded society, and beckoned in a quantity of lively and gay young persons with whom, as he was forbidden to work, he could play.

One of the persons with whom the Prince 'played' was Christopher Sykes, whose story shows Edward in a far less flattering light. Sykes was from a wealthy Yorkshire landowning family, and ten years older than Edward. In the words of his nephew and namesake, he was 'that age's [1870s] greatest fop and dandy . . . Dignity, majesty, and beautiful gloom . . . provide the keynote of his style.' The major weakness in his character was that 'he

The family of Queen Victoria in 1887, by Tuxen. A graphic demonstration of its ramifications through the royal courts of Europe (see p. 234 for key)

was an unredeemed snob; a snob, I fear, even by the standards of those intolerably snobbish days'. It was this that led to his downfall because it laid him open to the Prince of Wales, 'the Lord of London, with his inscrutable German eyes, his Tudor face, his gross pleasures'. Christopher Sykes's house was handy for Doncaster racecourse, where the St Leger was run each year, and the Prince came to stay regularly, and be entertained royally, as he also was at Sykes's house in Mayfair. Infinite pains were taken and the results were exquisite, and, for Sykes, ruinous. But the worst consequence was that Sykes became the butt of the royal sense of humour. His nephew describes how one night the Prince, 'moved by heaven knows what joyous whim', emptied a glass of brandy over his friend's head.

Christopher showed a rare thing: an excess of presence of mind. Not a muscle moved. Then, after a pause, he inclined to the Prince and said without any discernible trace of annoyance or amusement: 'As Your Royal Highness pleases.' The effect of this is recorded as being quite indescribably funny. Christopher dripped. Without a smile on his face he made no effort to mop up the tiny rivulets of spirit. The brandy had been poured by a royal hand.

The Prince flattered himself that he had made a discovery. Always an enthusiast for comedy, he had lighted on the greatest comic act of his time. He retained the child's pure enthusiasm which no amount of repetition can dim, and having enjoyed the great game of sousing Christopher once, he wanted to have it, in the touching way of infancy, 'again'. Well, royalty can command, and he had it again, he had it unnumbered times, he had it to the very end.

In place of the glass a full bottle was substituted, and another royal discovery was that even funnier effects could be conjured by pouring the precious liquid not on to his hair, but down his friend's neck. Amid screams of sycophantic laughter the Prince invented an entirely new diversion. Christopher was hurled underneath the billiard-table while the Prince and his faithful courtiers prevented his escape by spearing at him with billiard-cues. And there were further elaborations of the sousing theme. Watering cans were introduced into Christopher's bedroom and his couch sprinkled by the royal hand. New parlour games were evolved from the Prince's simple but inventive mind: while smoking a cigar he would invite Christopher to gaze into his eyes in order to see the smoke coming out of them, and while Christopher was thus obediently engaged, the Prince would thrust the burning end on to his friend's unguarded hand. His hat would be knocked off, the cigar would be

The Prince of Wales and friends: Christopher Sykes sits on the left, next to the Duke of Cambridge, who has mutton-chop whiskers

applied, the soda-water pumped over his head, and he would incline, and murmur: 'As your Royal Highness pleases.'

It must not be supposed, however, that Christopher sunk into a state of total degradation. He was not quite unmanned by his weakness. Following some unusually ferocious outburst, the Prince shouted at him in cacophonous good-fellowship: 'What d'ye take yerself for, Christopher, hey!' Christopher fixed upon him a stern look. 'For', he replied, 'Your Royal Highness's obedient, loyal and most tried servant.' It is said that the unexpected and awful solemnity of his tone reduced the Prince to silence for the moment, and to civilised behaviour for some weeks.

The routine went on through the 1880s, but by the end of that decade it had to stop, because Sykes's debts were huge. To give him his due, the Prince paid most of them, but it meant that Sykes could no longer be his host for the St Leger meeting. So, in September 1890 the Prince was to be found staying with a wealthy shipowner, Mr Arthur Wilson, at his house called Tranby Croft, near Doncaster. E. F. Benson tells what followed.

There was a large party in the house, most of whom, after dinner on the first evening of his visit, amused themselves with a game of baccarat. They played at a makeshift table, and during the progress of the game Mr A. S. Wilson, a son of the house, observed, so he thought, that his neighbour, Sir William Gordon-Cumming, Lieutenant-Colonel in the Scots Guards, was cheating. He whispered what he had seen to Mr Berkeley Levett, who was sitting on his other side, and who was a subaltern in the same regiment. They then both watched him, and again saw him cheating, withdrawing or augmenting his stake, under cover of his hand, according to the value of the cards he received. When the game was over Mr Wilson told his mother the same night what had occurred, and next morning also told his brother-in-law, Mr Lycett Green, who told his wife. There were thus five persons already who knew about it. As there would probably be a game of baccarat again on the second night, Mr A. S. Wilson procured a table of more convenient shape, on which it was hoped that cheating would be impossible.

So on this second night they sat down again to this damnable friendly game of baccarat: the Prince of Wales, as on the night before, took the bank. All five of the observers saw that on more than one occasion Sir William put his stake close to the line which is drawn round the table and separates the counters that are staked from those the player has in hand. If he got a good card, he supplemented his stake, if a bad one, he withdrew it or a portion of it. Their suspicions ceased to be suspicions at all, for they were convinced of the truth of them.

Their Royal Highnesses the PRINCE and PRINCESS of WALES accepting Caskets of TERRABONA TEA & COFFEE at the Company's depot at Constantinople (Olympia) on February the 8th 1894.

Princess Victoria of Wales

Princess Maud of Wales

Next day, after further confabulation, those who had watched told Lord Coventry and General Owen Williams, who was a close friend of Sir William Gordon-Cumming, what they had seen, and it was decided first to tell Sir William and then the Prince of Wales, who up to this point knew nothing whatever about what was going on. This was done. The Prince then interviewed Sir William in the presence of Lord Coventry and General Owen Williams, and afterwards those who had seen the unfair play. They all regarded a man who cheated at cards as a pest and an intolerable danger to his friends, and they determined to stop his card-playing. With the Prince's concurrence he was sent for and given a choice of two alternatives, and a declaration was written out in which he promised on his word of honour not to play cards for money again. If he would sign that, the committee promised him on their part that the matter would go no further, and that no one outside themselves should ever know about what had occurred. If he refused to sign, no such secrecy would be binding on them. Thereupon, though protesting his innocence, he signed the declaration, and it was witnessed by ten persons, of whom the Prince was the first signatory. The declaration was then put in the hands of the Prince, who sent it up to his Private Secretary in London, by whom it was placed, unopened, among his personal papers.

Some member (or possibly members) of this committee, who had obtained Sir William's signature on the definite promise that the matter would never be heard of again, must have given this pact away, for before the end of the year, he received an anonymous communication from

Scandal at Tranby Croft: a satirical print of the scene round the baccarat table which appeared in the magazine Truth *in 1891. At the left-hand end all eyes are on what Sir William Gordon-Cumming, seated second from left, is up to, but on the far side the Prince of Wales looks away. His host, Mr Arthur Wilson, peers through the curtains in his dressing-gown*

Paris, which showed him that the secrecy had been violated. A more odious treachery can hardly be conceived, and the victim of it brought an action for defamatory scandal against Mrs Arthur Wilson, Mr A. S. Wilson, Mr and Mrs Lycett Green and Mr Berkeley Levett. Sir William cited the Prince to appear as witness, and when the trial took place in the following June 1891, he took his place in the witness-box, and was examined by Sir Edward Clarke, counsel for the prosecution.

At the trial the evidence which most told against the plaintiff was the fact that he had signed this paper promising never to play cards again, and that was certainly most awkward, for this did not look like the conduct of an innocent man. His explanation was that, though innocent, he wished at any personal sacrifice to keep the Prince's name out of the affair. This view his counsel Sir Edward Clarke believed to be true. Sir Edward Clarke also argued that if the Prince of Wales and General Owen Williams had believed that Sir William had cheated they were bound to have reported it to the military authorities, and this they had not done. He inferred therefore that the Prince had not believed him guilty. A juryman, however, asked the Prince whether he believed him guilty or not, and the Prince said that he had no option, in the face of such support, to do otherwise. For the defence there was the impregnable argument that five persons, and those his friends, were sure they had seen him cheat on more than one occasion, and unless there was some monstrous and incredible conspiracy on their part, or unless they were all the victims of a collective hallucination, there was no explaining

it away. The verdict was exactly that which might have been expected, and the case was given for the defence.

The scandal that followed was colossal. If the Prince himself had been detected cheating, he could not have been more savagely sentenced. In particular all papers of a serious or religious turn, especially Church papers and Nonconformist papers, trumpeted their horror, like great moral elephants piously running amok.

The Times published a leader at the end of the trial, which, in conclusion, expressed regret that the Prince, as well as Sir William Gordon-Cumming, had not signed a declaration that he, too, would never play cards again. Though the Prince had known nothing about the cheating and the watching, it was he who drew the barrage fire of all these moralists, and publicly, owing to his position, he must be dumb.

His mother was able to make the Prince agree never again to play baccarat. However, she could not curb his enthusiasm for the Turf. Margot Asquith remembers him at Ascot, and then putting her at ease at a grand dinner party given by Winston Churchill's parents.

I had been presented to the Prince of Wales by Lady Dalhousie, in the Paddock at Ascot. He asked me if I would back my fancy for the Wokingham

Princess Alexandra on the Royal Yacht Osborne

Stakes and have a little bet with him on the race. We walked down to the rails and watched the horses gallop past. One of them went down in great form; I verified him by his colours and found he was called Wokingham. I told the Prince that he was a sure winner; but out of so many entries no one was more surprised than I was when my horse came romping in. I was given a gold cigarette-case and went home much pleased.

One night, when I was dining tête-à-tête with my old friend Godfrey Webb, in his flat in Victoria Street, my father sent the brougham for me with a message to ask if I would accompany him to supper at Lord and Lady Randolph Churchill's, where we had been invited to meet the Prince of Wales. I said I should be delighted if I could keep on the dress that I was wearing; as it was late and I had to get up early next day I did not want to change my clothes; he said he supposed my dress would be quite smart enough, so we drove to the Randolph Churchills' house together.

I was wearing a white muslin dress with transparent chemise sleeves, a fichu and a long skirt with a Nattier blue taffeta sash. I had taken a bunch of rose carnations out of a glass and pinned them into my fichu with three diamond ducks given me by Lord Carmichael, our Peeblesshire friend and neighbour.

On my arrival at the Churchills', I observed all the fine ladies wearing ball-dresses off the shoulder and their tiaras. This made me very conspicuous and I wished profoundly that I had changed into something smarter before going out.

The Prince of Wales had not arrived and, as our hostess was giving orders to the White Hungarian Band, my father and I had to walk into the room alone.

I saw several of the ladies eyeing my toilette and, having painfully sharp ears, I heard some of their remarks:

'Do look at Miss Tennant! She is in her night-gown!'

'I daresay no one told her that the Prince of Wales was coming . . . Poor child! What a shame!'

And finally a man said:

'There is nothing so odd as the passion some people have for self-advertisement; it only shows what it is to be intellectual!'

At that moment our hostess came up to us with a charming *accueil*. My father and I were much relieved at her greeting; and while we were talking the Prince of Wales arrived. The ladies fell into position, ceased chattering and made subterranean curtsies. He came straight up to me and told me I was to sit on the other side of him at supper. I said, hanging my head with becoming modesty and in a loud voice:

'Oh no, sir, I am not dressed at all for the part! I had better slip away, I had no notion this was going to be such a smart party . . . I expect some of

the ladies here think I have insulted them by coming in my night-gown!'

I saw everyone straining to hear what the Prince's answer would be, but I took good care that we should move out of earshot. At that moment Lord Hartington* came up and told me I was to go in to supper with him. More than ever I wished I had changed my dress, for now everyone was looking at me with even greater curiosity than hostility.

The supper was gay and I had remarkable talks which laid the foundation of my friendship both with King Edward and the Duke of Devonshire. The Prince told me he had had a dull youth, as Queen Victoria could not get over the Prince Consort's death and kept up an exaggerated mourning. He said he hoped that when I met his mother I should not be afraid of her, adding, with a charming smile, that with the exception of John Brown everybody was. I assured him with perfect candour that I was afraid of no one.

In the 1890s, just as today, the high point of the English racing year was the Derby. Lord Rosebery, shortly after becoming Prime Minister in 1894, won it with his horse Ladas. An American friend telegraphed: 'Many congratulations. Nothing left but Heaven.' He was wrong, because Rosebery won it again the following year, and in 1905. In 1896 it was the Prince of Wales's turn with Persimmon, which also won the St Leger and the Jockey Club Stakes that year. The win was immensely popular; the Prince's lapses over the years were forgotten in the general euphoria and

* Later the Duke of Devonshire.

Racing at Goodwood on the Sussex Downs, the last big fixture of each year's Season in July. The Prince of Wales stands in the centre with Adelina Patti, the opera singer (in red), sitting at his left. With her are pictured Gilbert, kneeling, and Sullivan, seated

113

his position in the heart of the nation firmly cemented. Marie Mallet reported on how it was taken at Balmoral:

The Queen was most interesting last night on the subject of racing and gambling and said she could not be pleased at the Prince of Wales's success at the Derby, though she did not wish to be unkind and she had telegraphed to him. She said it was the example she minded, not the actual fact and added, '*Il faut payer pour être Prince*' [to be a Prince has its price], then quoted what my grandfather had said the very last time she had seen him at Osborne when he was already very anxious about Uncle Charlie.

We are not told what the remark was, but Uncle Charlie was the 5th Earl of Hardwicke, the original Champagne Charlie and inventor of the glossy top hat. He was a friend of the Prince of Wales in the 1860s and was ruined in much the same way as Christopher Sykes. The day after the letter above, Marie Mallet added: 'We do not mention the Derby in public and the subject will be yet more taboo if HRH wins the Oaks.'

The Prince of Wales's eldest son Albert Victor, Eddy, the Duke of Clarence, was a dim figure in his own lifetime and the passage of the years has done nothing to illuminate him. He seems to have been lacking in intelligence and vitality, with a poor physique and a small head. He may or may not have been sighted at a male brothel largely staffed by telegraph boys in Cleveland Street in 1889. Lord Arthur Somerset, a son of the Duke of Beaufort and a major in the Royal Horse Guards who moved in the Prince of Wales's circle, was forced to flee abroad because of involvement in the Cleveland Street Scandal. But that hardly seems to justify the level of interest—if not downright interference—displayed in the subsequent court cases by powerful official figures. What is sure is that in 1890 the pressure to arrange a bride for the twenty-six-year-old Duke was mounting. His cousin Princess Alix of Hesse refused him—she was to marry the last Tsar instead; Princess Hélène of Orléans, another potential bride, was Catholic and could not change her religion. Eventually he became engaged to Princess May of Teck, only to die in 1892 before making it to the altar.

A letter from one of the Prince of Wales's equerries to the Queen's secretary Sir Henry Ponsonby casts a less than entirely melancholy light on the Duke of Clarence's funeral at Windsor. The Queen had placed the Castle at her son's disposal.

The Prince of Wales desires me to say that the harem of princesses was *not* locked into the further zenana [harem] pew closet, but the door got

Eddy – Albert Victor, Duke of Clarence, the Prince of Wales's eldest son – wearing the Balmoral tartan and a ludicrous badger sporran

jammed, and adds that they were none of them wanted at all. No ladies were to attend, and the Princess of Wales especially requested privacy — and to avoid meeting her Osborne relations. So they all came.

If Princess Beatrice was annoyed it cannot be helped and she must get over it — as she likes.

We are fairly comfortable in this most conveniently built house and most of our time is spent in a sort of game of 'post' or hide-and-seek, looking for and searching for each other and being hunted by servants who get lost.

We all admire various little economical thrifty dodges here. In the WCs — NEWSPAPER squares — there was one idea of sending them to Cowell [Master of the Household] in an unpaid envelope . . . And with a cup of tea — three lumps of loose sugar on the tray! ! It is admirable — and we now see why you are so rich.

The avalanche of telegrams and resolutions still pour in. One day over 1,700 telegrams! ! !

The best outcome from the Duke's death was that Alfred Gilbert, one of the

outstanding artistic figures of the late nineteenth century, was commissioned to design his monument. Gilbert was just completing the Shaftesbury Memorial, better known as the statue of Eros at Piccadilly Circus, and was at the height of his powers. A few years later, in 1896, Beatrix Potter said of him, 'I think he is very uneven, an eccentric individual. There was a story of someone finding him at lunch upon strawberries and treacle.' In the Windsor monument Eddy lies on his back, on a sarcophagus of Mexican onyx, in his uniform as a Xth Hussar; an angel holds an extravagant crown over his head, and a series of fantastic saints punctuates the grille surrounding the whole. Executed in bronze, brass, marbles, aluminium, ivory and semi-precious stones, it blends Pre-Raphaelite strains with Art Nouveau. As is so often the case with monumental sculpture, a nonentity became the pretext for a work of art.

Suitable royal wives were never two a penny and before long, Princess May had become engaged to Eddy's brother George, Duke of York. In July 1893 Lady Monkswell saw the wedding procession from a house in Piccadilly.

I could see the road cleared, and red-coated guards on either side nearly as far as Hyde Park Corner. The pavement was choked with people, many of the front row sitting on camp stools, others perched on the very sharp railings and in the trees. I felt quite proud of my country that we could do the thing so well. One of the first to pass was a detachment of Horse Artillery with six horses and the guns. There were I suppose almost a dozen State carriages with the footmen in gorgeous gold liveries hanging on like bees behind. Far away the most enthusiastic welcome was given to the old Queen. The Duchess of Teck was sitting backwards in the carriage with her. That was the best bit of the whole procession. Before her came fourteen or sixteen of the (horse) soldiers from Australia (Victorian) in pith helmets, then eight or ten of the Indian cavalry with their brown handsome faces, turbans, curious uniforms and swords—then the State Coach with four cream coloured ponies, their manes done up with quantities of purple ribbons, and purple reins. These ponies I believe are regular little devils, and to judge by the prodigious whisking of their long tails and tossing of their heads it was as much as the driver and walking grooms could do to keep them in anything like order.

The marriage of George, Duke of York, to Princess May, the future Queen Mary

117

I never saw such a crowd, quite good tempered, but oh, so hot. They were sitting about on the pavement or standing about in rows against the wall in the shade eating sandwiches or drinking ginger beer or fanning themselves; poor things.

The happy thought had occurred to me that we could go out late and see what we could of the illuminations. I started in some trepidation not knowing how far I should be allowed to drive. We were stopped about every 300 yds. by a policeman but the magic words 'Member of Parliament' opened the way. I waited some ten minutes in the star-lit [Westminster] Palace Yard for Bob in the warm lovely night. When he came out we took advantage of our privileges in a thoroughly improper manner and made ourselves perfectly intolerable to a vast number of people by driving up Parliament Street, Leicester Square, Regent Street and Oxford Street. People *did* call out occasionally — 'get down', 'turn them out' — and I quite sympathised with them. The coachman was in a horrid fright lest they should turn over the carriage. However we drove boldly on until we were stopped by a particularly stern policeman in Oxford Street — such a scene, thousands and thousands of orderly well behaved people, girls in shirts and straw hats, husbands carrying babies, and the wife leading another little child.

Queen Victoria's eldest daughter Vicky was Empress of Germany for only a hundred days before her husband Frederick died of cancer in 1888. We may laugh at the ballad that was on sale in the London streets soon afterwards, but it turned out to be only too accurate.

He will be missed by many now that he has left this shore,
Because he was a man for peace, he was not the one for war.
No one can say that while he lived but what he did his best
To keep the country around him in quietness and rest.
Her dear Empress Victoria will take it much to heart,
For she was a fond and loving wife, and now they have to part.
Now he has been called away, there is not the slightest doubt,
But what the people in the country will be very much put about.
By what is being said now, and what has been said before,
It seems very plainly there means to be a war.

Frederick and Vicky's son became Emperor Wilhelm II. The democratisation of Germany along liberal British lines that Wilhelm's father intended was anathema to Bismarck, the creator of the German Empire. Wilhelm was entirely happy to fall in with Bismarck's nationalistic and autocratic ideas, and indifferent to any hurt he inflicted on his mother in

118

The future Kaiser Wilhelm II, one of Queen Victoria's grandsons, before the death of his father

the process. Queen Victoria took strong exception to her grandson's behaviour, but swallowed her feelings in the interests of good relations between Britain and Germany. Wilhelm came regularly for the Cowes regatta, and Lord Wolseley describes a dinner for him at Osborne nearby in August 1890.

We dined in a tent joining on to the house. After the dinner the Queen stood up and proposed the Emperor's health, which we drank: the band had been ordered to play, and the piper not to pipe when this was done. There was a pause: no band. The Queen angry: messenger sent for the band to play—all still standing, when in burst the pipes, blowing hard at 'Scots wha hae', or something of that sort. The Queen furious, calling out to stop that piper. Piper turned back and his wind-bag silenced. No

*The arrival of Tsar
Nicholas II and his
wife Alix to stay at
Balmoral in 1896*

band, so we all sat down. The Duke of Connaught began long explanation across the table to the Queen, who was very angry, but in the middle of it in again burst the irrepressible piper and his infernal lament over some old Highland cow that had 'been stolen away'. It was too comical, and everyone burst out laughing, the Emperor setting the example, and the Queen joining in it. The Emperor was very jolly all day, full of life and fun, with great reality in all he does or says.

1890 was the year in which Bismarck was forced to resign, unable to restrain Wilhelm any longer from increasingly wild talk. He remarked, 'the Kaiser is like a balloon: if you don't keep fast hold of the string, you never know where he'll be off to.' Unlike his grandmother, the Emperor had, in E. F. Benson's words, 'a prodigious imagination but no common sense that could be lit up by it; his imagination flared on to an empty void where he beheld only the Brocken spectre of himself clad in shining armour'. In 1891 Wilhelm came on a state visit to England and the verdicts on him were much less flattering than Wolseley's. Arthur Balfour: 'He certainly has enormous energy, self-confidence, and interest in detail; all very good things in their way: while the fact that he firmly believes he has a mission from Heaven, though this will very possibly send him and his country ultimately to Hell, may in the meantime make him do considerable deeds on the way there.' Augustus Hare saw 'a fat young man [he was thirty-one] with a bright good-humoured face, though apparently never free from the oppression of his own importance, as well as of the importance of his dress, which he changes very often in the day'. Lord Salisbury's daughter, Gwendolen, reported that when she was discussing British parliamentary government with him, he ended by saying, 'Thank God, I am a tyrant.' In 1892 Sir Henry Ponsonby wrote:

The Emperor is certainly a most excitable man and proposes all sorts of wild schemes for England . . . Lord Salisbury observes, if he is in this excitable mood he may be dangerous and that a few hours' conversation with the Queen can appease him. So he hopes HM will see him at Darmstadt, which she does not at all want to do. She said to me 'No, no, I really cannot go about keeping everybody in order.'

In April 1894 the Queen was told of the engagement of her granddaughter Alix of Hesse (she who had spurned the hand of 'Eddy', Duke of Clarence) to the Tsarevich Nicholas. He was the eldest son of Tsar Alexander III and his wife, the former Danish Princess Dagmar, sister of Princess Alexandra of Wales. No wonder the bearded Duke of York (George V) and the bearded Tsar Nicholas II (as the Tsarevich became in October) were mistaken for each other. In 1896 Nicholas and Alix paid a visit to Britain, which coincided with what Lady Monkswell called 'a great day all over the world. Today [23 September] the dear old Queen has reigned longer than any British Sovereign. What a day of emotion for her. The young Emperor and Empress, our Princess Alix, came to her at Balmoral and she sat waiting to receive them in a room full of trophies from Sebastopol! It was the anniversary of the fall of Sebastopol.' This Russian stronghold in the Crimea had fallen to the British and French in 1855.

Queen Victoria drawn in four lines, by Alma-Tadema

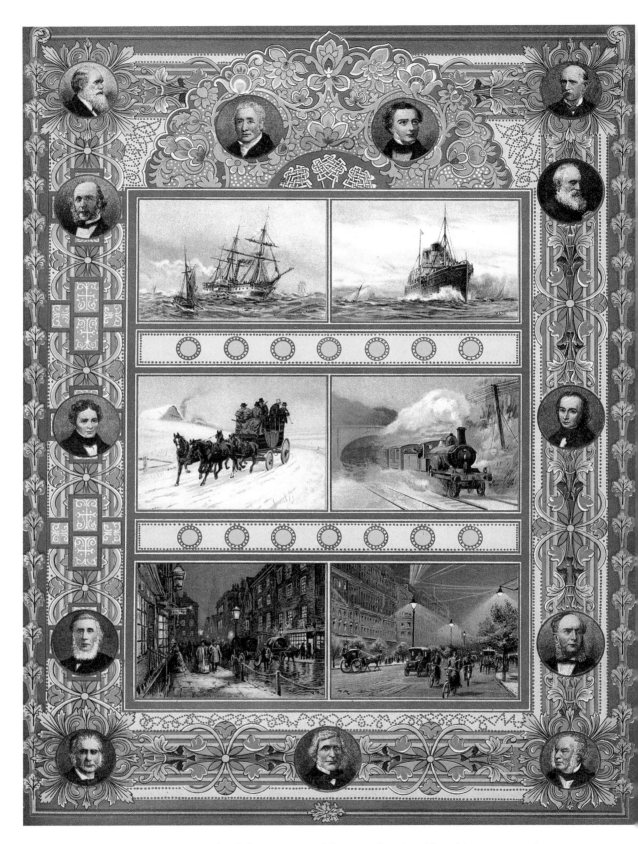

A Diamond Jubilee souvenir celebrating the scientific achievements and improvements in transport of Victoria's reign

Science, Technology, Transport and Sport

'In 1895 the novelist Henry James acquired electric lighting; in 1896 he rode a bicycle; in 1897 he wrote on a typewriter; in 1898 he saw a cinematograph.' Thus Professor Norman Stone cleverly brings together some of the benefits of science and ingenuity from this period. Gaslight, steam, iron and the telegraph were being challenged by electricity, internal combustion, steel, and such invisibles as radio waves and X-rays. There were new uses for newish materials, such as rubber and celluloid, whether to make tennis and golf balls, or tyres and film. Speeds went up and increasing distances were covered. Jerome K. Jerome took a rather whimsical view of 'Progress' in his memoirs:

It was the typewriter that led to the discovery of woman. Before then, a woman in the City had been a rare and pleasing sight. The tidings flew from tongue to tongue, and way was made for her. The telephone was hailed as a tremendous advance towards the millennium. The idea then current was that, one by one, the world's troubles were disappearing. But for a long while, it saved time and temper to take a cab and go round and see the man. Electric lighting was still in the experimental stage; and for some reason got itself mixed up with Bradlaugh* and atheism: maybe, because it used to go out suddenly, a phenomenon attributed by many to the wrath of God. A judge of the High Court was much applauded for denouncing it from the Bench, and calling for tallow candles.

The lurking dangers of science were espied by the older generation even in such unlikely subjects as botany. In 1893 Lady Emily Lytton reported a

---

* Elected an MP in 1880, Charles Bradlaugh was not admitted to the House of Commons until 1886, because he refused to take the oath on the grounds of his atheism. He made a habit of challenging the Almighty in public to strike him dead within the next minute, and then pulling out his watch to time Him.

conversation between her sister Betty and their mother's first cousin, Lady Ampthill:

Lady A.: Did you see the Flower Show at the Temple? It was so beautiful, such lovely begonias.

Betty: I myself think those double flowers are always hideous, but of course it was a wonderful show. I went with Emily, who is a botanist, and she told me many amazing things about flowers.

Lady A.: Oh, a botanist, is she? I suppose she doesn't go in for it very thoroughly.

Betty: Oh, indeed she does. Very thoroughly indeed. She does nothing else now.

Lady A.: But I believe botany is very improper when you go in for it thoroughly?

Betty: It is just the fun of it. Emily tells us such amazing things about the sexes of the plants. All sciences are improper when you go in for them thoroughly.

Lady A.: How about astronomy?

Betty: I mean things of the earth, earthy.

Lady A.: I do not think there would be anything improper about geology.

Betty: I don't know, but there has been a lot written and told about it. Darwin, you know, has written a lot about it, and then there are footprints, we are told a lot about those.

Consumption is a disease we particularly associate with nineteenth-century Europe, whether it is Keats dying in Rome or expiring operatic heroines like Violetta in La Traviata *and Mimi in* La Bohème. *The German scientist Robert Koch isolated the tubercle bacillus in 1882 and in 1890 he announced a cure for tuberculosis. The Empress Frederick (Vicky) wrote to her mother, Queen Victoria, about it.*

Koch's cure still, as you can imagine, excites the intensest curiosity, excitement and interest and I am afraid that people whose expectations have been unduly raised by the tremendous noise in the Press will be doomed to many a disappointment. There has, as yet, not been time to effect a perfect cure, and no one can say with *certainty* that this can be done. There is so much still to be studied and worked out that it is wrong to form a hurried judgement one way or another. The discovery is most important and most extraordinary, but whether it will be universally adopted as a cure remains to be seen, and must be patiently waited for.

In 1892 a message was sent by radio for the first time. The following account is from the Spectator.

Mr W. H. Preece, Chief Engineer and Electrician to the Post Office, has been trying to test at Cardiff the idea which has for some time past been floating among experts in electricity that it was possible to convey a message by electricity from point to point without the intervention of any wire; and this is the result he has obtained. He put up a wire a mile long on the coast near Lavernock, a little south of Cardiff, and a shorter wire on Flatholm, a little island three miles off in the Bristol Channel. He fitted the latter wire with a 'sounder' to receive messages, and sent a message through the former from a powerful telephonic generator. That message on the mainland was distinctly heard on the island though nothing connected the two—or, in other words, the possibility of a telephone between two places unconnected by wire was conclusively established. This of itself is a wonderful triumph of applied science, for henceforward communication can be established, without laying cables, between any shore and any neighbouring lighthouse, or between the shore and a ship approaching it, or between a besieged city and friends outside who cannot use any other means of communication. But these are trivialities compared with the possibilities opened by the *method* of transmission. That message did not travel through earth or water or even air, but was transmitted through ether by waves of a certain, probably unusual, magnitude. That is, it flew through a medium independent, not only of human volition or energy, but of this planet, the medium which, so far as we know, fills all space—the medium through which light reaches us, say, from the star Sirius. In other words, Mr Preece had generated a wave of electricity which, for aught he knows, or anyone else knows, may have the power of conveying sound as far as the wave of ether which conveys light, that is, for a distance which human thought does not cover, and which is for human purposes the equivalent of infinity.

In 1896 Lady Monkswell saw some X-rays and had their medical application brought home to her.

Old Dr Kiallmark was here today and showed us the first private photograph I have ever seen by these wonderful 'Röntgen rays' [X-rays]. A woman had squeezed a needle right into the palm of her hand. The hand was photographed, the rays shone through the flesh and only put in the bones, and there, sure enough, was the needle with the point broken off lying close to one of the bones. As old Dr Kiallmark said, he might have

Two cantilever arms of the Forth Bridge about to be joined

been grubbing after that needle with a probe for six months and never have found it, and now he knows where it is as well as if he saw it.

Kenneth Clark, in his book Civilisation, *suggested that the comparative weakness of architecture in the Victorian period was due in part to the 'strongest creative impulse of the time' going into engineering instead. Many of the outstanding feats of the engineers were in the field of bridge building, and the 1890s saw the completion of two quite spectacular examples: the Forth Bridge in 1890 and the Tower Bridge in 1894.*

The Forth Bridge, allowing the main east coast railway line to continue directly northwards from Edinburgh, is the more admired in our austere days, thanks to its honesty in leaving the materials from which it is built undisguised and unadorned. (At the time, William Morris called it 'the supremist specimen of ugliness'.) Tower Bridge, across the Thames, however, is about as far removed from such 'truth to materials' as it could be, seeking instead, via its two flamboyant Gothic towers, to complement the neighbouring Tower of London, in a well-mannered way. (The Builder *magazine condemned them as 'architectural gimcrack on a large scale'.)*

In fact, both bridges were made possible by the use of steel, rather than the ironwork which had been the basis of so many earlier Victorian engin-

126

Tower Bridge under construction, 1892

eering triumphs. It was steel that allowed the massive cantilever construction of the Forth Bridge, with its upper lattice girders in tension and its lower tubular members in compression. It was steel from which the Tower Bridge's two opening leaves or bascules, each weighing 1,200 tons, were constructed, as well as the hydraulic-powered equipment which raised or lowered them at two feet a second. Their object was to enable big ships still to reach the upper part of the Pool of London and unload in the heart of the City. In both cases the strength and flexibility of steel could be harnessed thanks to the hydraulic riveting techniques perfected by Sir William Arrol, a remarkable innovator as well as an enlightened employer.

The moving spirit behind the Forth Bridge was Sir John Fowler, who had been responsible for the construction of many railways, including the first London Underground line—the Metropolitan. There were two names that resonated among those responsible for Tower Bridge: the engineers John Wolfe Barry—son of Sir Charles Barry who had built the Houses of Parliament—and Henry Marc Brunel—son of Isambard Kingdom Brunel of the Great Western Railway and the Great Eastern steamship. The Forth Bridge was opened by the Prince of Wales, who drove in the last, gilded, rivet; and Gustave Eiffel was among those *present. Its 145 acres of steelwork, kept free of rust by 29 painters, enabled 542,000 trains to cross the Firth of Forth in its first twenty years. Tower Bridge was also inaugurated by the Prince of Wales and was soon opening an average of eighteen times a day, although the walkways at the top, for pedestrians to use when the bascules were raised, were shut in 1910 due to lack of use. E. F. Benson's mother, as wife of the Archbishop of Canterbury, attended the opening of Tower Bridge, 'rather pleased with herself and her smart landau with its pair of black horses and her coachman in a wig. But that little bubble of pride was soon pricked for her by a ribald voice in the crowd which shouted " 'Ullo! 'Ere comes the Queen's cook!" '*

The innovation which perhaps spread quickest and which had the greatest impact at this time, thanks to the way it enlarged peoples' worlds, was the safety bicycle. This is the machine that we know, chain-driven with two wheels of the same size. Until the mid 1880s bicycles had been penny-farthings ('spiders'), but these now rapidly disappeared, helped on their way out by the introduction of the Dunlop pneumatic tyre for safety cycles in 1888.

Jerome K. Jerome

The first bicycles were nicknamed 'spiders'. The front wheel was anything from fifty to sixty inches in diameter and was joined to a diminutive back wheel by a curved steel bar, shaped like a note of interrogation. Their riders had to be youths of skill and courage, or woe betide them. They wore tight-fitting breeches and short jackets that ended at the waist.

It was my nephew, Frank Shorland, who first rode a safety bicycle in London. Young Frank was well known as an amateur racer. He believed in the thing the moment he saw it, and agreed to ride his next race on one. He was unmercifully chaffed by the crowd. His competitors, on their tall, graceful 'spiders', looked down upon him, wondering and amazed. But he won easily, and from that day 'spiders' went out of fashion.

The coming of the 'safety' made bicycling universally popular. Till then, it had been confined to the young men. I remember the bitter controversy that arose over the argument: 'Should a lady ride a bicycle?' It was some while before the dropped [cross] bar was thought of, and so, in consequence, she had to ride in knicker-bockers: very fetching they looked in them, too, the few who dared. But in those days a woman's leg was supposed to be a thing known only to herself and God. 'Would you like it, if your sister showed her legs? Yes, or no?' was always the formula employed to silence you, did you venture a defence.

In Battersea Park, any morning between eleven and one, all the best blood in England could be seen, solemnly pedalling up and down the half-mile drive that runs between the river and the refreshment kiosk. But these were the experts—the finished article. In shady bypaths, elderly countesses, perspiring peers, still in the wobbly stage, battled bravely with the laws of equilibrium; occasionally defeated, [they] would fling their arms round the necks of hefty young hooligans who were reaping a rich harvest as cycling instructors: 'Proficiency guaranteed in twelve lessons'. Cabinet ministers, daughters of a hundred earls might be recognised by the initiated, seated on the gravel, smiling feebly and rubbing their heads.

It was rumoured that when Lady Londonderry (p.43) came to Battersea Park to learn to ride, she brought two footmen with her to prop her up. In her memoirs published in 1935 Helena Swanwick remembered the harassment to which women cyclists were subjected, from men perhaps frightened by such an obvious display of independence.

Near Manchester the boisterous mill-hands would play pranks on me, linking arms across the road to upset me. The only way to cope with this

Cycling along Rotten Row in Hyde Park, 1895

was to avoid looking at them and, putting down my head, charge full tilt,
when they would scatter. In London, bus drivers were not above flick-
ing at me with the whip, and cabmen thought it fun to converge upon
me from behind. I was pulled off by my skirt in a Notting Hill slum, and
felt a bit scared till a bright idea struck me. I said to the loutish lad who
had seized my handle-bar, 'I say, they seem rather a rough lot here. I
wonder whether you would kindly help me out?' He instantly clutched
my arm with his other hand, and bustling along with great dignity,
shouted, 'Nah then! Mike room for the lidy, can'tcher?' He saw me
through, and helped me to re-mount with the recommendation, 'Cut
away nah, quick!' And I did.

My long skirt was a nuisance and even a danger. It is an unpleasant
experience to be hurled on to stone setts [cobbles] and find that one's
skirt has been so tightly wound round the pedal that one cannot even get
up enough to unwind it. But I never had the courage to ride in breeches
except at night.

Modern traffic may make the horse-drawn days seem attractive, but Jerome K. Jerome's descriptions of the hazards of the hansom cab and the two-horse bus soon disabuse one, and perhaps explain why he was enthusiastic enough about early motoring to take part in the first-ever London-to-Brighton Run in 1896.

London traffic at Holborn Circus in the 1880s, including hansom cabs

Hansoms were the most uncomfortable contrivances ever invented. To get into them, you grabbed at two handles, one jutting out from the splash-board and the other just over the wheel, and hauled yourself up on to a small iron step. If the horse made a start before you got further, you were carried down the street in this position, looking like a monkey on a stick. If you had not secured a firm hold, you were jerked back into the gutter, and the cab went on without you: which was safer, but even less dignified. Getting out was more difficult. A false step landed you on all fours, and your aunt or your sister, or whatever it might happen to be, stepped on you. To enter or alight without getting your hat knocked off by the reins was an art in itself. The seat was just big enough for two. It was high, and only long ladies could reach the floor. The others bobbed up and down with their feet dangling. The world always thought the

Bayswater Omnibus,
by George Joy

worst, but as often as not one put one's arm round her purely to prevent her from slipping off. There was a trapdoor in the roof. Along dim-lit roads, one noticed the cabman holding it open, and driving with his head bent down. A folded window could be let down by the driver to protect you from the rain. It was called the guillotine. That was another thing that always knocked your hat off—and then it hit you on the head. Most people chose the rain. If by any chance the horse slipped, then the 'apron' doors would fly open and you would be shot out into the road—minus, of course, your hat. Another experience that could happen to you in a hansom was the breaking of the belly-band; and then the whole thing tilted up; and you lay on your back with your legs in the air and no possibility, if you were a lady, of getting at your skirts.

The old two-horse bus, one is glad has disappeared, if only for the sake of the horses. It had straw inside and a little oil lamp that made up in smell what it lacked in illuminating power. It carried twelve inside, and fourteen out—ten on the knife-board, and two each side of the driver. The seats by the driver were reserved for acrobats. You caught a swinging strap and sprang on to the hub of the front wheel, leapt from there on to the trace-pin and then with a final bound gained the footboard. The 'knife-board' was easier of attainment. You climbed up a fixed ladder, the

rungs a foot apart. The only real danger was from the man above you. If he kicked out you were done. There was no bell. Passengers stopped the bus by prodding the conductor with their umbrellas. The driver wore a mighty coat with flapping capes, and wrapped a rug round his legs before strapping himself to his seat.

On a morning in 1896, a line of weird-shaped vehicles, the like of which London had never seen before, stood drawn up in Northumberland Avenue outside the Hotel Metropole. They were the new horseless carriages, called automobiles, about which we had heard much talk. The law, insisting that every mechanically propelled vehicle should be preceded by a man carrying a red flag, had expired the day before; and at nine o'clock we started for Brighton. We were fifth in the procession. Our driver, a large man, sat perched up on a dicky just in front of us, and our fear throughout the journey was lest he should fall backwards, and bury us. An immense crowd had gathered, and until we were the other side of Croydon it was necessary for mounted police to clear a way for us. At Purley, the Brighton coach overtook us, and raced us into Reigate. By the time we reached Crawley, half our number had fallen out for repairs and alterations. We were to have been received at Brighton by the mayor and corporation and lunched at the Grand Hotel. It was half-past three before the first of us appeared. At lengthening intervals some half a dozen others straggled in to be received with sarcasm and jeers. We washed ourselves—a tedious operation—and sat down to an early dinner. All the vested interests of the period—railway companies; livery stable keepers, and horse dealers; the Grand Junction Canal; the Amalgamated Society of Bath-chair Proprietors, and so forth, were, of course, all up in arms against us. One petition, praying Parliament to put its foot down upon the threatened spoiling of the countryside, was signed 'Friends of the Horse'. It turned out to be from the Worshipful Company of Whipmakers. Some credit is due to the motorists of those days. It was rarely that one reached one's destination. As a matter of fact, only the incurable optimist ever tried to. The common formula was: 'Oh, let's start off, and see what happens.' Generally, one returned in a hired fly.

At first, we wore masks and coloured goggles. Horses were terrified when they met us. We had to stop the engine and wait. I remember one old farmer with a very restive filly. Of course we were all watching him. 'If you ladies and gentlemen', he said, 'wouldn't mind turning your faces the other way, maybe I'd get her past.'

Bicycling and motoring, already touched on, could be regarded as sports rather than just modes of transport. If they are added to the more purist sports that were started or came to prominence around this time, then the list is very impressive. Invented in the 1870s (when it was called Sphairistike), by the 1880s lawn tennis was all the rage. Indeed, the character of the aesthetic poet Bunthorne in Gilbert and Sullivan's Patience *was originally to have been called the Revd Lawn Tennison. Part of the game's popularity arose because women played it from the very first. Women also increasingly took up golf. Arthur Balfour, while admitting in his memoirs that 'golf underwent an expansion which amounted almost to a revolution' at this period, was too modest to say that his own enthusiasm for it was a major reason for this. He was a very fashionable figure and whatever he did caught the public eye. Lady Warwick also claimed that 'his fondness for golf started the weekend habit. It needed only one prominent man to start using the country at weekends to make Society remember it had beautiful country homes.' In 1892 Lady Emily Lytton and her sister Betty were staying at Arthur Balfour's home, Whittinghame, in East Lothian where, as he said, thanks to its sand and short turf, 'the southern shore of the Firth of Forth is largely made up of ideal golf courses in a marvellous succession'. But Emily's initiation into the game sounds not to have been on one of them. Betty was married to Arthur Balfour's brother, Gerald.*

Lady Emily Lytton

The Tennis Party, *by Sir John Lavery*

I always thought the game dull to watch, but it is still more dull to play. To see Betty play is a very delicious sight. She tries to be so very serious over it, and puts on the regular golfing expression, swings her club in quite a professional way, and after a huge effort only succeeds in knocking up a large bit of turf and never touches the ball. I being a beginner hardly ever hit the ball, and never sent it where it ought to go. After we had dawdled round the house in this way for about half an hour, Betty and I decided we preferred a short sharp walk to golf. I have always heard of Scotch air as life-giving. The only effect it has had upon me at present is to give me a bad cold. The air is certainly colder than anywhere else, if that is a merit.

The second half of the century saw the evolution of cricket into the game which we can recognise today. The dominating figure throughout the period was W. G. Grace; the son of a Gloucestershire doctor, he was himself a doctor and had three brothers who were cricketing doctors. Here is Neville Cardus, the greatest of writers on cricket:

Picture him on guard against Spofforth, the forked lightning threatening the great oak . . . Picture him as he runs over the earth to bowl, shaking it: 'an enormous man, rushing to the wicket, both elbows out, a black beard blowing on both sides of him, a huge yellow cap on the top of a dark, swarthy face'. He was the most dominating man ever seen on a cricket field. He was shaggy, gigantic.

When Grace was 'not out' at lunch at Lord's the London clubs quickly emptied and the tinkle of hansom cabs along the St John's Wood Road had no end . . . It has been told that outside a cricket field it was often possible to read the following sign: 'Admission threepence; if

Dr W. G. Grace plays, admission sixpence' . . . In those days the line between county and country cricket was slenderly drawn . . . Once in a rustic game Grace had scored twenty or so runs. He played in these modest engagements with all the keenness he put into a Test match . . . On this occasion he was brilliantly stumped by the local wicket-keeper. Grace had played forward and lifted his right toe only for a fraction of a second. 'H'zat?' shrieked our yokel wicket-keeper, in a panic of triumph, seeing himself rendered immortal by his cleverness against 'The Champion'—'H'zat?' 'Not hout!' replied the umpire without loss of time. 'Not hout—and look'ee here, young feller, the crowd 'as come for to see Dr Grace, and none of your monkey tricks.'

Early in the 1895 season, when he was aged forty-seven, Grace achieved his hundredth century with an innings of 288, during which he only allowed four balls to pass the bat, and snow settled on his beard. In May he also became the first to achieve 1,000 runs a feat only equalled again in 1927.

If asked, most people would say that Arthur Conan Doyle's greatest contribution to the sum of human happiness was his creation of Sherlock Holmes. But the following passage from his memoirs might give them pause.

I can claim to have been the first to introduce skis into the Grisons division of Switzerland. It was in 1894 that I read Nansen's account of his crossing of Greenland, and thus became interested in the subject of skiing. It chanced that I was compelled to spend that winter in the Davos valley, and I spoke about the matter to Tobias Branger, a sporting tradesman in the village, who in turn interested his brother. We sent for skis from Norway, and for some weeks afforded innocent amusement to a large number of people who watched our awkward movements and complex tumbles. The Brangers made much better progress than I. At the end of a month or so we felt that we were getting more expert, and determined to climb the Jacobshorn, a considerable hill just opposite the Davos Hotel. In ascending you shuffle up by long zig-zags, the only advantage of your footgear being that it is carrying you over snow which would engulf you without it. But coming back you simply turn your long toes and let yourself go, gliding delightfully over the gentle slopes, flying down the steeper ones, taking an occasional cropper, but getting as near to flying as any earth-bound man can. In that glorious air it is a delightful experience.

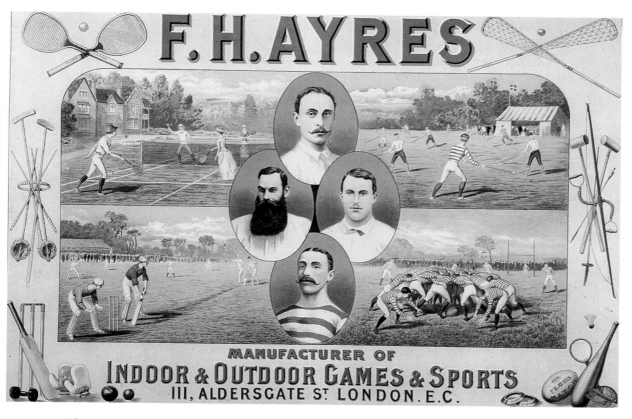

F. H. AYRES

MANUFACTURER OF
INDOOR & OUTDOOR GAMES & SPORTS
111, ALDERSGATE ST. LONDON. E.C.

The sports favoured by the leisured classes centred on fish, fowl and horses. Margot Asquith brilliantly brings back the flavour of a hot day at the races, when Fred Archer, perhaps the best jockey of all time, was riding.

A sports equipment maker's advertisement. The spade-bearded W. G. Grace is one of the four sportsmen in the centre

One day, at Ascot, some of my impecunious Melton [hunting] friends—having heard a rumour that Archer, who was riding in the race, had made a bet on its result—came and begged me to find out from him what horse was going to win. It was a grilling day; most men had handkerchiefs or cabbages under their hats; and the dried-up grass in the paddock was the colour of pea-soup. I saw Fred Archer standing in his cap and jacket with his head hanging down, talking to a well-groomed, under-sized little man, while the favourite—a great, slashing, lazy horse—was walking round and round with the evenness of a metronome. I went boldly up to him and reminded him of how we had cannoned at a fence in the VWH.* Fred Archer had a face of carved ivory, like the top of an umbrella; he could turn it into a mask or illuminate it with a smile; he had long thin legs, a perfect figure and wonderful charm. He kept a secretary, a revolver and two valets and was a god among the gentry and the jockeys. After giving a slight wink at the under-sized man, he turned away from him to me and, on hearing what I had to say, whispered a magic name in my ear ... I was a popular woman that night in Melton.

* The country hunted by the Vale of White Horse, a pack of foxhounds.

With the technical improvements to shotguns since the 1850s—now breachloading, hammerless ejectors firing 'smokeless' cartridges—game shooting reached something of an apogee. First the Liberal politician Sydney Buxton explains why driven grouse shooting is so exciting, then Timothy Eden portrays his choleric, highly strung, perfectionist father, Sir William Eden, shooting pheasants. (It was he who, when one of his guests asked if they were to shoot hen as well as cock pheasants, replied, 'Yes! Shoot hens! Shoot everything! Shoot the Holy Ghost if he comes out!')

Sydney Buxton

The dreary London pavement and the exhausted London atmosphere have at last been left behind. The gentle exercise refreshes the body; the lovely, far-stretching, bracing, limpid surroundings soothe the brain and rest the eye. There you stand, waiting for the birds to come. At first somewhat careless and casual, the while guns are loaded, cartridges and paraphernalia conveniently disposed, sods altered, foothold trodden level, and speculation indulged in with your loader as to the likelihood of the particular butt being a lucky one. Far away on the distant hill, a tiny white speck or two mark the line of beaters; but all is as yet still and motionless. Suddenly a shot from a neighbouring butt at a bird or a pack prematurely flushed puts every sense and nerve on the alert.

Then a further interval of suspense. The faintly distinguished flapping of his flag by a distant flanker, shows that birds have been started. And soon some moving black dots are distinguishable, circling round in the distance, or a flash of wings is caught as birds top a mound and disappear into the hollow. The heart beats rapidly, the gun is grasped more tightly, the foothold is made more secure. 'Will they come to me . . . yes . . . no . . . no . . . yes . . . and no' again, as they curve up to the right and stream over a neighbouring butt some way off. A grouse drops, and the quick eye takes in the fall of the bird an appreciable time before the slower sound of the shot reaches the duller ear.

And now it is 'yes', and the fresh pack come well over the butt, high and fast. A rapid and proper selection is made, the aim is straight and true—pleasure and satisfaction reign supreme.

Timothy Eden

If Eden were shooting well, then all was rosy, smiles were on every face, chaff and good humour waited at the cover side. On such a day it was an education and a pleasure to be with him; he was a delightful companion, a humorous, indulgent master, a joy to watch for the grace and quickness

Boulter's Lock, by Edward Gregory. The increased enthusiasm for outdoor pursuits saw a boating craze sweep England, resulting in scenes like this and books such as Three Men in a Boat

Going North, *by George Earl. The scene at King's Cross station, terminus for the main East Coast line to Scotland, in August at the start of the grouse shooting season. Besides the pointers and setters, there are golf clubs, an early tennis racket, and fishing tackle in evidence. The man on the carriage roof is filling the oil lamps*

of his movements. An onlooker once counted thirty-eight pheasants to his gun out of a possible forty, all streaming from a tall beech wood on the slope of a hill, as high as one could wish to see them, and scarcely a wounded bird amongst the fallen. It was not lack of skill which prevented him from taking his place amongst the few crack shots in England, but the ease with which he was thrown off his balance. A bad beginning, tobacco smoke in his face on the way from one stand to another, a woman fidgeting behind him or getting in his way, a fumble by the loader, some innocent's unfortunate remark, a sneeze to make him jump just as he was going to fire—each and any of these were enough to spoil his day, to set him missing and screaming and cursing, making himself and all around him miserable. 'I'll break these bloody guns!' he yelled one day, holding the offending weapon high above his head in both hands. 'Don't do that, Sir William,' called out his neighbour, greatly daring: 'give them to me!'

140

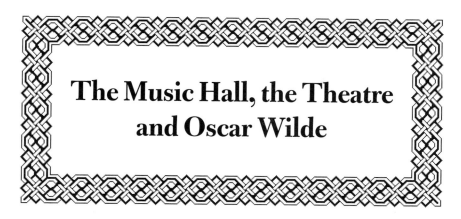

The Music Hall, the Theatre and Oscar Wilde

As the country's wealth increased, public transport from the suburbs and within towns improved, electric light was gradually introduced, and the appetite for something more than home entertainment grew fast. Music halls and theatres sprang up in great numbers to satisfy it. Max Beerbohm describes the delights to be found in the former.

I was a callow undergraduate, in my first Christmas vacation [in 1890]. I had been invited to dine at the Café Royal by my brother Julius, whose age was twice as great as mine; and after dinner he proposed that we should go to the Pavilion Music Hall, where a man called Chevalier had just made his début, and had had a great success. I was filled with an awful, but pleasant, sense of audacity in venturing into such a place, so plebeian and unhallowed a den, as a music hall; and I was relieved, though slightly disappointed also, at finding that the Pavilion seemed very like a theatre, except that the men around us were mostly smoking, and not in evening clothes, and that there was alongside of the stalls an extensive drinking-bar, of which the barmaids were the only — or almost the only — ladies present, and that the stage was occupied by one man only. One and only, but great: none other than the Great MacDermott, of whom I had often heard in my childhood as the singer of 'We Don't Want To Fight, But, By Jingo, If We *Do*'. And here he was, in the flesh, in the grease-paint, surviving and thriving, to my delight; a huge old burly fellow, with a yellow wig and a vast expanse of crumpled shirt-front that had in the middle of it a very large, not *very* real diamond stud. And he was still belligerent, wagging a great imperative forefinger at us across the footlights, and roaring in a voice slightly husky but still immensely power-ful a song with the refrain 'That's What We'd Like To Do!' In Russia there had been repressive measures against Nihilists, and Mr Joseph Hatton had written a book entitled 'By Order of the Czar' — a book that created a great sensation. And in consequence of it the Great MacDermott had

The Gallery of the Old Bedford, *by Walter Sickert. This was a famous London music hall*

been closeted with the Prime Minister; nor did he treat the interview as confidential. I remember well some words of his song.

' "What would you like to do, my Lord?"
I asked Lord Salisburee'——

But the fierce mood was short-lived. There arose in the firmament another luminary. Albert Chevalier, as new as MacDermott was old, came shining forth amidst salvoes of fervid expectation. A very elastic and electric little creature, with twists and turns of face and body and voice as many as the innumerable pearl buttons that adorned his jacket and his breeches. Frankly fantastic, but nevertheless very real, very human and loveable in his courtship of 'Arriet by moonlight, or in his enjoyment of the neighbours' good wishes as he drove his little donkey-

The comedian Dan Leno on a song-sheet cover

chaise along the Old Kent Road. I was at that time too young to appreciate the subtleties of the technique that he had acquired and matured on the legitimate stage. But in later years I knew enough to realise that he was becoming rather a slave to these subtleties. He was no longer content to merge his acting in the singing of a song. He acted outside the song, acted at leisure between the notes, letting lilt and rhythm go to the deuce. But his composition of words and music never became less good. There was always a firm basic idea, a clear aspect of human character. 'My Old Dutch', 'The Little Nipper', 'You Can't Get a Roise out o' Oi', and the rest of them, still live for that reason . . .

Gus Elen defied the conventions only by the extreme, the almost desperate glumness of his demeanour, and the bitterness of what he had to say, on a stage where cheeriness against all odds was ever the resounding key-note. Immensely acrid was the spirit of his ' 'E Dunno where 'e Are'

143

Le Lion Comique, *by Sickert.* Lions comiques *were a particular type of music-hall performer, and one of the most famous of them was The Great MacDermott, described by Max Beerbohm on p.141*

and of his 'Well, it's a Grite Big Shime'; but even these were mild in comparison with the withering pessimism of a later song of his . . . 'What's the good of ennyfink? Why, nuffink!'

Very different was the philosophy of Dan Leno. Fate had not smiled on him, his path was a hard one, he was beset by carking troubles and anxieties, he was all but at his wits' end, the shadow of the workhouse loomed, but there was in his little breast a passion of endurance, and a constant fount of hope, that nothing could subdue. His meagre face was writhen with care, but the gleam in his eyes proclaimed him undefeatable. He never asked for sympathy: he had too much of Cockney pride to do that; but the moment he appeared on the stage our hearts were all his. Nature had made him somehow irresistible. Nor do I remember any one so abundant in drollery of patter. He was, by the way, the inaugurator of patter. In his later years he hardly sang at all. There was just a perfunctory gabble of a stanza and a chorus, and the rest was a welter of the spoken word—and of imaginative genius . . .

Mr Harry Freeman, dear man, sounded no depths, and scaled no heights of sentiment, and indeed had no pretensions of any kind, except a thorough knowledge of his business, which was the singing of songs about Beer, about the Lodger, about being had up before the Beak, about the Missus, about the seaside, and all the other safest and surest themes. He never surprised one. He never disappointed one. He outstood in virtue of being a perfect symbol and emblem of the average. I delighted in him deeply. I think he had a steadying influence on me. To this day, whenever I am over-excited, or am tempted to take some unusual and unwise course, I think of Harry Freeman . . .

I ceased to attend the Halls because the virus of 'Variety' had come creeping in: conjurors, performing elephants, tramp-bicyclists, lightning calculators, and so on, and so forth. The magic had fled—the dear old magic of the unity—the monotony, if you will—of song after song after song, good, bad, and indifferent, but all fusing one with another and cumulatively instilling a sense of deep beatitude—a strange sweet fore-taste of Nirvana.

The Empire in Leicester Square was one of the biggest London music halls, famous for the elaborate ballet routines of its chorus line. It was to be the scene of Winston Churchill's first public speech.

In my last term at Sandhurst my indignation was excited by the Purity Campaign of Mrs Ormiston Chant. This lady was a member of the London County Council and in the summer of 1894 she started an active movement to purge our music halls. Her attention was particularly directed to the promenade of the Empire Theatre. This large space behind the dress circle was frequently crowded during the evening performances, and especially on Saturdays, with young people of both sexes, who not only conversed together during the performance and its intervals, but also from time to time refreshed themselves with alcoholic liquors. Mrs Ormiston Chant and her friends made a number of allegations affecting both the sobriety and the morals of these merrymakers; and she endeavoured to procure the closing of the promenade and above all of the bars which abutted on it. The controversy aroused keen public interest; but nowhere was it more searchingly debated than among my Sandhurst friends. We were accustomed to visit this very promenade in the brief leave allowed to us twice a month from Saturday noon till Sunday midnight. We were scandalised by Mrs Chant's charges and insinuations. We had never seen anything to complain of in the behaviour of either sex.

A compromise was reached and the bars were partially separated from the promenade by canvas screens, but with gaps left so that it was still possible to move between them.

I was myself filled with scorn at the hypocrisy of this nefarious peace. I had no idea in those days of the enormous and unquestionably helpful part that humbug plays in the social life of great peoples dwelling in a state of democratic freedom.

On the first Saturday night after these canvas obstructions had been placed in the Empire promenade [they] were examined with attention and soon became the subject of unfavourable comment. Then some young gentleman poked his walking-stick through the canvas. Others imitated his example. Naturally I could not hang back when colleagues were testifying after this fashion. Suddenly a most strange thing happened. The entire crowd numbering some two or three hundred people became excited and infuriated. They rushed upon these flimsy barricades and tore them to pieces. The authorities were powerless. Amid the cracking of timber and the tearing of canvas the barricades were demolished, and the bars were once more united with the promenade to which they had ministered so long.

In these somewhat unvirginal surroundings I now made my maiden speech. Mounting on the debris and indeed partially emerging from it, I addressed the tumultuous crowd, finishing up by saying 'You have seen us tear down these barricades tonight; see that you pull down those who are responsible for them at the coming election.' These words were received with rapturous applause, and we all sallied out into the square brandishing fragments of wood and canvas as trophies or symbols.

Sir Henry Irving was the dominating figure on the stage from the 1870s onwards. Together with the actress Ellen Terry and aided by his manager Bram Stoker, remembered these days as the author of Dracula, *Irving electrified audiences at the Lyceum Theatre. Max Beerbohm sums up his strengths and weaknesses, then Ellen Terry throws light on his enigmatic character.*

Max Beerbohm

It was as a producer of Shakespeare that Irving was great in management. He was the first man to give Shakespeare a setting contrived with archaic and aesthetic care . . . Of course spectacle may be overdone. Irving may sometimes have overdone it; but he always overdid it beautifully . . . As philosopher or king, poet or prelate, he was matchless. One felt

A theatrical poster of Henry Irving as Faust

that if Charles the Martyr, Dante, Wolsey, were not precisely as he was, so much the worse for Wolsey, Dante, Charles the Martyr.

Ellen Terry

He is the first to be perfect in his words at rehearsal of any new play. For 'a good poet (and actor) is *made* as well as born'—as old Ben Jonson wrote. He sees things at a flash, *after* pondering upon them for weeks! He studies, and studies, and then *has inspiration*. He very seldom will rehearse his part *quite* as he is going to do it at night, but he maps it all out, and scientifically goes through it with the others so that they may see what he intends to do, but he reserves all passion of the part until the evening performance.

A thousand little things prove he has no idea of his own beauty—personal beauty. He uses his very fine hands unconsciously, except in what are called 'character' parts. One day he said: 'Physical gifts of voice, beauty, etc. are the best equipment for an actor, and I believe I am the only actor on record who has succeeded in spite of having none of these

Henry Irving as Cardinal Wolsey

gifts.' He said it very earnestly, almost triumphantly, quite believing it. I grant his intellectuality dominates his other powers and gifts, but I have never seen in living man, or picture, such distinction of bearing. A splendid figure, and his face very noble. A superb brow; rather small dark eyes which can at moments become immense, and hang like a bowl of dark liquid with light shining through; a most refined curving Roman nose, strong and delicate in line, and *cut clean* (as all his features); a smallish mouth, and full of the most wonderful teeth, even at fifty-five; lips most delicate and refined—firm, firm, firm—and with a rare smile of the most exquisite beauty, and quite-not-to-be described kind. (He seems always ashamed of his smile, even in very private life, and will withdraw it at once in public.) His chin, and the line from the ear to chin is firm, extremely delicate, and very strong and clean defined. He has an ugly ear! Large, flabby, ill-cut, and pasty-looking, pale and lumpy. His hair is superb; beautiful in 1867, when I first met him, when it was blue-black like a raven's wing, it is even more splendid now (1895) when it is liberally streaked with white. It is rather long, and hangs in lumps on his neck, which is now like the neck of a youth of twenty! His skin is very pale, delicate, refined, and stretched tightly over his features. Under the influence of strong emotion, it contracts more, and turning somewhat paler, a grey look comes into his face, and the hollows of his cheeks and eyes show up clearly.

Never have I seen such hands, 'in form and moving how *express* and admirable'. He always makes them up for the stage very brown.

I think it is not quite right in him that he does not care for anybody much. (I think he has always cared for me a little, very little, and has had passing fancies, but he really *cares* for scarcely anyone.) Quiet, patient, tolerant, impersonal, gentle, *close*, crafty! Crafty sounds unkind, but it is H. I. 'Crafty' fits him. The best in him is his patience, his caution, his strong, practical will, and his gentle courtesy. His worst is his being incapable of caring for people, sons, friends, anyone, and his lack of enthusiasm for other people's work, or indeed for anything outside *his own* work. It has caused him, I should say, a great loss of happiness, yet the *concentration* has achieved results. If it could be possible for him to take this infinite pains for *another*, he would be a perfect being, but self-concentration spoils the porridge. He has faults, but still such an overbalancing amount of virtues, that he is quite one of the best and most remarkable men of his time.

In 1893 Lady Monkswell went to see Irving in Tennyson's play, Becket:

The scene opened with a really enchanting view, Becket and Henry II playing chess on the battlements of an old Norman castle—you could really feel the blue sky above them, and out beyond was a wide stretch of country and a winding narrow river, no doubt exactly like what Normandy really is. I have never seen Irving to such advantage, the dress suited him so admirably; first the gorgeous archbishop's robes, most magnificent; and then the long sackcloth tunic and the longer black cloak and hood—'the ordinary habit of the Black Canons of the Augustine Rule'.

After Becket refuses to seal the document the knights spring upon him up the steps with their swords drawn, and three or four of the most infuriated jump on the table and run across it—most life-like. Then just at the end of the scene the big doors open and you see Becket standing under the low arch with the crowd behind him. I was particularly pleased with the last scene but one where Becket sits in a room in Canterbury monastery waiting for the knights to come and murder him, the organ playing in the distance and the bell ringing. The last scene in the north transept of Canterbury seemed to me extremely like the place—a thick pillar and arch, and staircase behind, and red painted windows

which shone. In the dim light the old man stands alone by the pillar, the crowd of frightened monks has fled in disorder, you feel the knights are close at hand. They enter in complete armour: Becket seems to be so helpless, and yet not afraid. After they have murdered him (quite deliberately) they slash their swords up and down in a sort of transport of rage and cry in hoarse voices 'King's men, King's men'—It makes one's blood run cold.

Lady Emily Lytton was evidently not one of Irving's fans: 'Cardinal Wolsey's part suited Irving in some ways, as he had no opportunity of ranting, but he made as many dreadful faces as he could, and stalked about the stage in an absurd way. He talks as if it was such an awful effort to get his words out that it is quite painful to sit and hear him. I longed to give him a good shake.' Edward Burne-Jones, on the other hand, was entranced by him in the role: 'How nobly he warmed up the story of the old religion to my exacting mind. I shall think always of dying monarchy in his Charles—and always of dying hierarchy in his Wolsey. How Protestant and dull all grew when that noble type had gone! I can't go to church till red cardinals come back nor to Court till trumpets and banners come back.'

W. Graham Robertson trained as a painter, but made his mark as a theatrical designer. The powers of observation which his training developed were put to good use when he came to write his reminiscences of the studios, boudoirs and dressing rooms of the 1890s: Time Was. *In recalling his first meeting with her in 1887, he tries to pin down the charm of Ellen Terry and in particular discusses her in the role of Lady Macbeth as seen in the famous painting by John Singer Sargent (p. 154). Ellen Terry then has her own say about the part.*

W. Graham Robertson

A fairer vision than Ellen Terry, then at the zenith of her loveliness, cannot be imagined: she shone with no shallow sparkle or glitter, but with a steady radiance that filled the room and had the peculiar quality of making everybody else invisible.

From after experience I feel sure that she was in act of whispering to her hostess, 'Now don't you bother about me and I'll just slip in without being noticed and sit down somewhere'—a feat which might have been performed with equal ease by the sun at noonday.

W. Graham Robertson and his toothless dog Mouton, by Sargent. The dog 'was always allowed one bite by Sargent before work began . . . Being an amateur model, I was easily entrapped into a trying pose . . . It was hot summer weather and I feebly rebelled against the thick overcoat. "But the coat is the picture," said Sargent. "You must wear it." '

Ellen Terry

Though I could only secure a few words I at once fell completely under the matchless charm of her personality; the stuffy room and the jigging music faded, leaving only Ellen Terry, who might have stepped in from some dim garden, her arms full of lavender and lad's-love and bringing with her a freshness, a breeze from the open sky.

Of Our Lady of the Lyceum, as Oscar Wilde used to style her, what a series of wonderful pictures lives in the memory. As Portia I think she must have realised almost everyone's ideal—she *was* Portia; as Beatrice she realised something so far above *my* ideal that I could hardly recognise the character, for I have the bad taste not to admire Beatrice.

About the Lady Macbeth of Ellen Terry there was much diversity of opinion because she did not conform to the accepted Siddons tradition, but her view of the character was an entirely legitimate and logical one and supported by every line of the part. Driven on by love and ambition for her husband she determines at all costs to sweep away the one obstacle that bars his way to power; she sees no further than the murder of Duncan and until this is accomplished she is steel and adamant, allowing no thoughts of pity or honour to weaken her purpose. The murder done, her strength fails; she cannot support Macbeth in his lying tale or act out the scene of hypocritical grief; she faints and is carried away and thenceforward is but a weary, broken creature, flashing into action for a moment at the interrupted banquet but almost at once sinking back into apathy.

As Lady Macbeth her appearance was magnificent: long plaits of deep red hair fell from under a purple veil over a robe of green upon which iridescent wings of beetles glittered like emeralds, and a great wine-coloured cloak, gold embroidered, swept from her shoulders.

The effect was barbaric and exactly right, though whence the wife of an ancient Scottish chieftain obtained so many oriental beetles' wings was not explained, and I remember Oscar Wilde remarking, 'Judging from the banquet, Lady Macbeth seems an economical housekeeper and evidently patronises local industries for her husband's clothes and the servants' liveries, but she takes care to do all her own shopping in Byzantium.'

Ellen Terry

Sargent's picture is almost finished, and it is really splendid. Burne-Jones yesterday suggested two or three alterations about the colour which Sargent immediately adopted, but Burne-Jones raves about the picture.

It (*Macbeth*) is a most tremendous success, and the last three days' advance booking has been greater than ever was known, even at the Lyceum. Yes, it is a success, and I am a success, which amazes me, for never did I think I should be let down so easily. Some people hate me in it; some, Henry among them, think it my best part, and the critics differ, and discuss it hotly, which in itself is my best success of all! Those who don't like me in it are those who don't want, and don't like to read it fresh from Shakespeare, and who hold by the 'fiend' reading of the character . . . Oh, dear! It is an exciting time! . . . I wish you could see my dresses. They are superb, especially the first one: green beetles on it, and such a cloak! The photographs give no idea of it at all, for it is in colour that it is so splendid. The dark red hair is fine. The whole thing is Rossetti—rich stained-glass effects. I play some of it well, but, of course, I don't do what I want to do yet. Meanwhile I shall not budge an inch in the reading of it, for that I know is right. Oh, it's fun, but it's precious hard work for I by no means make her a 'gentle, lovable woman' as some of 'em say. That's all pickles. She was nothing of the sort, although she was *not* a fiend and *did* love her husband. I have to what is vulgarly called 'sweat at it', each night.

Ellen Terry as Lady Macbeth, by Sargent. Oscar Wilde saw her arrive at Sargent's studio in Tite Street, Chelsea. 'The street that on a wet and dreary morning has vouchsafed the vision of Lady Macbeth in full regalia seated in a four-wheeler can never again be as other streets: it must always be full of wonderful possibilities.'

One of the most explosive nights in the theatre was provided in 1893 by the opening of Arthur Wing Pinero's play The Second Mrs Tanqueray, *with an unknown actress, Mrs Patrick Campbell, in the title role. (Much later, her friend Bernard Shaw was to write the part of Eliza Doolittle in* Pygmalion *for her.) First, W. Graham Robertson describes discovering her, and then Mrs Patrick Campbell relates her experience of the production.*

W. Graham Robertson

George Alexander was completely absorbed in a new play by Pinero which he was going to produce. By all who had read it it was thought to be a very daring, nay, dangerous experiment. Nowadays, I suppose, it would be regarded as a bright little entertainment for children in the holidays, but then it was surprising, as it dealt in candid fashion with the situation of a respectable middle-aged man married to a lady whose former profession was, in those unenlightened days, still regarded as a formidable barrier to social success. Florence Alexander and I were deputed to make a round of the theatres in search of her,* but she remained hidden. One evening we set dutifully out for the Adelphi to inspect Miss Evelyn Millard. She was very beautiful, very gentle, very sweet, about as like Paula Tanqueray as a white mouse is like a wild cat; another evening was evidently to be spent in vain—when the scene changed and the wicked woman of the play came on.

She did not look wicked—a startling innovation. She was almost painfully thin, with great eyes and slow haunting utterance; she was not exactly beautiful, but intensely interesting and arresting. She played weakly, walking listlessly through the part, but in one scene she had to leave the stage laughing: the laugh was wonderful, low and sweet, yet utterly mocking and heartless. Florence Alexander and I both realised that there before our eyes was the ideal Paula Tanqueray. If she would only move, speak, look, above all, laugh like that the part would play itself. Neither of us knew the lady, who, the programme stated, was a Mrs Patrick Campbell.

Mrs Patrick Campbell

The reality of the play after the melodrama I had striven with at the Adelphi made my heart bound with joy, and no doubt I showed some intelligent and vivid appreciation, though I did not at this reading for a moment understand what Paula's life was. Did I ever grasp it in my interpretation: I wonder?

* In search of an actress to play Mrs Tanqueray.

Mrs Patrick Campbell

Both author and manager were worried and anxious at rehearsals. I heard afterwards that more than one management had refused *The Second Mrs Tanqueray*, considering the play too *risqué*.

I was an amateur so far as trained technique went. And I was wilful, self-opinionated, strangely sensitive, impatient, easily offended, with nerves strained by illness. At first they treated me as a child that must be taught its ABC. I was given no free rein. My passionate longing for beauty, my uncontrollable 'sense of humour'—or whatever it was that made me quickly recognise the ludicrous and artificial—was snubbed. A snub shattered me, unless at the moment my spirits were high enough to give me the courage to go one better.

At last the rehearsal of the third act reached the point where the stage direction reads: 'She sits at the piano and strums a valse.' Now my mother had never allowed any of her children to strum. She insisted on all art being treated with reverence, and impressed upon us that the piano was not a toy. The painful trifling known as strumming was forbidden in our home. Many a time have I known the piano locked—someone had been punished.

I played rather well and with a passionate love of touch and tone, which gained me my scholarship at the Guildhall School of Music; but I am not a musician in the true sense of the word.

I sat down to the piano hesitatingly, asking twice to be excused, until I had prepared something suitable. A voice from the stalls: 'We would like to hear whether you can play.' This offended me. Holding my book in my right hand, with my left I played beautifully—and with impertinence—a piece written by a girlfriend of mine. This moment changed the whole temper of the rehearsals. Those who listened knew that my playing must be the outcome of serious study and some understanding of art; above all that my playing would invest the part of 'Paula' with not a little glamour.

Mr Pinero and Mr Alexander were in the stalls; at last from the darkness an expressionless voice said, 'That will do, Mrs Campbell, we will go on with the rehearsal, please!' From that moment there was a difference. It seemed to me that Mr Pinero especially treated me with more confidence.

Then came the first of the two dress rehearsals, no one being permitted into the auditorium except Mr Pinero, and he was to sit alone in the dress circle with a lantern, a notebook, and a pencil. I implored him not to speak to me, and I would play the part for him. I kept my word, and to that dark, silent house and that solitary man I poured out my 'secret' with the fire and feeling of my temperament and imagination. I wanted to plead for Paula, I wanted her to be forgiven and remembered. I tried from the beginning to lift Paula a little off the earth, to make her not merely a neurotic type; to give her a conscience, a soul.

A second dress rehearsal was called. This time there were other people sitting in the stalls, scattered here and there. With some strange professional instinct of self-preservation, I knew I was too nervously exhausted to act the part again before the first night. I was spiritless, flat, dull, and everyone was depressed.

Then came the first night. 'How unnecessarily noisy the audience is,' I thought, as the play proceeded. After the scene at the end of the second act, it irritated me not a little. I thought they would have been more silent if they had been more deeply moved and interested.

Gradually the audience realised the tragedy of poor Paula—how her love for Aubrey Tanqueray had lit up the dark recesses of her nature, illuminating her soul—how in her struggle to subdue her jealousy, her boredom—to forget—to begin life again—she at last, in that terrible moment when she looks at herself in a mirror, and cries out that her past life is written indelibly on her face, and that her husband will always see it there—realises in a flash her life has unfitted her for ever to grasp and hold the simple happiness which her love for Aubrey puts within her reach. Her soul is horror stricken, and because her higher control has been rendered helpless, she, in her anguish, destroys her body.

The ovation when the curtain fell, incredible as it may seem, was lost upon me. The tremendous applause stupefied me, and I never for a moment thought a share of it was mine.

Crowds of people flocked on to the stage; shy and terrified I ran up to my dressing-room, dressed quickly, picked up my dog, and went back to my lodgings, worn out by fatigue.

The next morning my two children climbed into my bed. I told them all about the applause, and that I was sure the play would have a long run; we had breakfast in bed for a treat, where later Mrs Alexander found us. She asked me why I had left the theatre, and told me I had made a great personal success and my name famous.

Lillie Langtry may have been an actress in her later days, but really she was 'famous for being famous', her beauty causing crowds in Hyde Park and winning the closest of attentions from the Prince of Wales.

W. Graham Robertson

I was wandering in Rotten Row one Sunday morning when I became aware of a commotion among the solemn promenaders; a crowd collected, women scrambled on to chairs to get a better view, from all directions people converged towards some hidden centre of interest. As the hustle surged past me I suppose I must have stood open-mouthed and obviously interrogative, for a total stranger gripped my arm in passing and panted: 'Mrs Langtry—run!'

I had heard of Mrs Langtry and I ran. Being very slender and compressible, I wriggled easily through the struggling throng and peeped into the clear space of enchanted ground at its midst.

There, conversing with a tall and distinguished man (I feel sure that he was tall and distinguished, though naturally I did not look at him), stood a young lady in pale cream colour. Her back was towards me, but, as she talked, her head in its little close bonnet drooped slightly forward like a violet or a snowdrop—— Good heavens! the Jersey Lily, the Venus Annodomini, the modern Helen.

Sarah Bernhardt (right) and Lillie Langtry

Never since the days of the Gunnings* had such universal worship been paid to beauty. The Langtry bonnet, the Langtry shoe, even the Langtry dress-improver, were widely stocked and as widely bought; photographs of Mrs Langtry papered London. Yet the Jersey Lily of the Eighties remained very simple in her dress and manner, her grey eyes looked gravely out at a city in undignified prostration at her feet; she made no parade of her beauty; indeed, none was required.

'The Lily is so tiresome,' once sighed Oscar Wilde to me. 'She *won't* do what I tell her.'

'How wrong!' said I with mental reservations.

'Yes,' murmured Wilde, 'I assure her that she owes it to herself and to

* Famous, eighteenth-century, fashionably beautiful sisters.

us to drive daily through the Park dressed entirely in black in a black victoria drawn by black horses and with "Venus Annodomini" emblazoned on her black bonnet in dull sapphires. But she won't.'

For many Sarah Bernhardt was the greatest actress of her age, not merely in her native France, but in England too, where she had regular seasons. W. Graham Robertson became her friend and steeped himself in her mystique. Before his analysis of her, he recalls their first meeting.

I bought a beautiful pair of new gloves and set forth, consoling myself with the reflection that I could not look a greater fool than I felt.

I well remember her first coming to me with outstretched hands across the great empty room, her russet hair loosely wisped up, her long robe of cream-coloured velvet falling over an underdress of mauve silk gathered into a silver girdle. Several other people were there, but I have forgotten all about them, as one generally did in the presence of Sarah. Old Madame Guèrard I know was one, who always lived and travelled with her and had been much more to her than her own mother throughout her life.

My hostess placed me beside her at table where I sat tongue-tied and gaping like a fish. I remember that the conversation fell upon the roles in life which we should each choose to play.

'I should like to be a queen,' said Sarah at once.

'My dear child,' protested Madame Guèrard, 'what people do you think would ever stand you? You would find yourself with your head off in a week.'

Sarah reflected. 'Yes,' she said gravely, 'I suppose I should, but'— brightening up—'I should have had lots of other people's heads off in that week.'

Was Sarah Bernhardt beautiful? Was she even passably good looking? I have not the slightest idea. Beauty with her was a garment which she could put on or off as she pleased. When she let it fall from her she was a small woman with very delicate features, thin lips, a small beautifully modelled nose, hooded eyes of grey-green shadowed by a fleece of red-gold hair, strong slender hands, and a manner full of nervous energy. But when she would appear beautiful, none of these details were to be perceived; her face became a lamp through which glowed pale light, her hair burned like an aureole, she grew tall and stately; it was transfiguration.

Towards the end of her supreme period critics began to carp at what had charmed them for so long and to say that the much-hymned 'golden voice'—a soft chant, little above a whisper, yet of a penetrating and bewildering sweetness—was a trick commonly practised by High Church curates, that it was no natural tone but a false voice.

Who ever said that it was not?

Sarah Bernhardt herself told me that she had hit upon this false voice as a means of saving her natural voice, which was, in her youth, easily exhausted; that she achieved it—as does the curate—by pitching the voice up in the head and producing it through the nose, and that, by alternating it with her natural utterance, she could come safely through long tirades which otherwise would have left her speechless.

But to produce a false voice and to use it beautifully are two different things; with the curate it is sing-song and dull monotony, from the lips of Sarah Bernhardt it was the cooing of doves, the running of streams, the falling of soft spring rain. And its carrying power!

I remember calling at the stage door of some theatre in London to leave a message and asking the doorkeeper whether the act was finished or if Madame Sarah was still on the stage. The man merely said, 'Listen'. I listened, and up from the far-distant stage, along passages, up stair-ways, through heavy swing doors, came the murmuring chant of the *voix d'or*. No other voice was audible; when the voice of Sarah ceased there was silence till it began again. 'Rum, ain't it?' commented the stage door-keeper.

'Phèdre'* was undoubtedly her greatest part. She brought all her powers to bear upon it and gave herself up to it in a way that was unusual with her.

I have often been amazed by her double consciousness when acting; have found her at the close of a great scene weeping bitterly, panting, half fainting from the emotions through which she had apparently passed, yet with her mind centred upon some subject far away from the part she had been playing, as, for instance, some curious figure among the audience which had attracted her notice and to which she had been giving her almost undivided attention.

But Phèdre she approached in a different spirit. She would speak little during the day before a performance and, if she could help it, not at all between the acts. She seemed actually to become the passion-tossed queen and to realise nothing outside her mimic kingdom.

Once I met her at the wings as she tottered off, hardly able to stand, after the terrible scene in which she urges Hippolyte to kill her. Her hands were covered with blood—blood was streaming down her white robes.

'What is the matter? How have you hurt yourself?' I cried.

She stared at me with unseeing eyes. 'I have not hurt myself,' she said slowly. 'Nothing is the matter. What do you mean?'

* In Racine's play of the same name.

I pointed to the rapidly spreading stains and, with an effort, Sarah seemed to emerge from Phèdre and looked in astonishment at her bleeding hands.

'It was the sword,' she said at last. 'It must have been Hippolyte's sword. I seized it and held it—it has cut deep into my hands—but I felt nothing at all—nothing.'

This species of ecstasy, this careful husbanding of her strength always ceased with her last great scene of passion: the final act, though she played it as exquisitely as the rest, took nothing out of her.

'I have only to die,' she told me. 'The last act is nothing at all'; and when her call came, she would cry 'Allons mourir' and dance gaily off to her death.

Her art always made for beauty. I have seen many actresses agonise through the last moments of *La Dame aux Camélias** with heart-rending fits of coughing and sick-room symptoms in full play.

Sarah passed lightly and mercifully over these details and struck an infinitely deeper and more touching note by the portrayal of an overwhelming happiness.

The change that came over the face of the dying woman when she heard of her lover's coming was a nightly miracle to which I never got accustomed. I have often watched it from the side, at about four yards' distance, but it was no trick of the stage.

There was first a quick look at the bearer of the news, then the haggard face began to glow, the skin tightened all over it, smoothing away every line and giving an effect of transparency lit from within, the pupils of the eyes dilated, nearly covering the iris and darkly shining, the rigid lips relaxed and took soft childish curves, while from them came a cry that close at hand sounded no louder than a breath yet could be heard in the uttermost corner of the theatre. The frail body seemed to consume before our eyes in the flame of an unbearable joy and to set free the glorified and transfigured spirit.

In 1892 plans were afoot for Sarah Bernhardt to perform in a new play at an almost-new theatre, the Palace at Cambridge Circus in London. It had been built in 1890 for Richard D'Oyly Carte by Thomas Collcutt, architect of the Savoy Hotel and of the Imperial Institute, that permanent memorial in South Kensington of the Queen's Golden Jubilee. D'Oyly Carte's profits from the Gilbert and Sullivan operas paid for both the Savoy and the Palace, with its curved terracotta exterior and marble, alabaster and onyx interior. The author of the play, which he had chosen to write in French, was Oscar Wilde. As W. Graham Robertson points out, Wilde

* This play by Alexandre Dumas was the basis of Verdi's opera *La Traviata*.

took considerable liberties with the Bible version: this is not 'Salomé, the schoolgirl, just home for the holidays, showing off her accomplishments at her mother's bidding, all unwitting of what "that one dance of her feet" would bring forth, an arresting figure', but 'Salomé, the wanton, dancing away the life of the man who scorned her and gloating over his severed head, a theatrical commonplace'. In spite of his reservations, he and Oscar Wilde

had often talked over its possible production together. 'I should like,' he said, throwing off the notion, I believe, at random, 'I should like every-one on the stage to be in yellow.'

It was a good idea and I saw its possibilities at once—every costume of some shade of yellow from clearest lemon to deep orange, with here and there just a hint of black—yes, you must have that—and all upon a pale ivory terrace against a great empty sky of deepest violet.

'A violet sky,' repeated Oscar Wilde slowly. 'Yes—I never thought of that. Certainly a violet sky and then, in place of an orchestra, braziers of perfume. Think—the scented clouds rising and partly veiling the stage from time to time—a new perfume for each new emotion!'

'Ye-es,' said I doubtfully, 'but you couldn't air the theatre between each emotion, and the perfumes would get mixed and smell perfectly beastly and—no, I don't think I care for the perfume idea, but the yellow scheme is splendid.'

However, when Sarah accepted the play and was to put it on at once during her short London season, there was no time for the yellow scheme and she had to do what she could with the material ready to her hand. I was called in to help and advise.

For Sarah I had designed a golden robe with long fringes of gold, sus-tained on the shoulders by bands of gilt and painted leather which also held in place a golden breastplate set with jewels. On her head was a triple crown of gold and jewels and the cloud of hair flowing from beneath it was powdered blue.

'*C'est la reine Hérodias qui a les cheveux poudrés de bleu*,' Oscar had read, to be at once interrupted by Sarah, 'No, no; Salomé's hair pow-dered blue. I *will* have blue hair!'

'By the by,' said I to Sarah. 'The dance.'

'What about it?'

'I suppose you will get a *figurante** to go through it, won't you? veiled, of course, and with your blue hair——'

'I'm going to dance myself,' said Sarah.

'*You* are going to dance the Dance of Seven Veils?'

* Member of the ballet chorus.

Enter Herodias, one of Aubrey Beardsley's illustrations for Oscar Wilde's Salomé. *The figure in the foreground is a caricature of Wilde*

'Yes.'

'But—but how?'

'Never you mind,' said Sarah, with her enigmatic smile—and to this day I cannot imagine what she intended to do. For, alas, our labours were vain and *Salomé*, banned by the Censor, was never seen upon the boards.

It was curiously thoughtless of Oscar Wilde not to have applied earlier for a licence which, in those days, he should have known was very unlikely to be granted, and Sarah, thinking of her wasted time and trouble, felt no little indignation. She had no notion that the play was yet in the balance or would not have undertaken the production, and the verdict of the Censor came as a complete surprise to her; nevertheless, she put aside her wrath to condole very kindly with the poet in his disappointment.

Such carelessness on Oscar Wilde's part was symptomatic of a major change in his behaviour by 1892. The days in the early 1880s when, as W. Graham Robertson said, he held the 'position of high priest of aestheticism, won in drawing-rooms by persistently making a fool of himself', were long over, but so too were the much more sober years later in that decade, when he edited Woman's World *magazine and was writing* The Happy Prince *and* Dorian Gray. *Arthur Conan Doyle met him in the late 1880s at a dinner arranged by an agent of the American publishers Lippincott.*

Wilde to my surprise had read *Micah Clarke* and was enthusiastic about it, so that I did not feel a complete outsider. His conversation left an indelible impression upon my mind. He towered above us all, and yet had the art of seeming to be interested in all that we could say. He had delicacy of feeling and tact, for the monologue man, however clever, can never be a gentleman at heart. He took as well as gave, but what he gave was unique. He had a curious precision of statement, a delicate flavour of humour, and a trick of small gestures to illustrate his meaning, which were peculiar to himself. The effect cannot be reproduced, but I remember how in discussing the wars of the future he said: 'A chemist on each side will approach the frontier with a bottle'—his upraised hand and precise face conjuring up a vivid and grotesque picture.

The result of the evening was that both Wilde and I promised to write books for *Lippincott's Magazine*—Wilde's contribution was *The Picture of Dorian Gray*, a book which is surely upon a high moral plane, while I wrote *The Sign of Four*, in which Holmes made his second appearance. I should add that never in Wilde's conversation did I observe one trace of coarseness of thought, nor could one at that time associate him with such an idea.

Early in 1891 Wilde had met and become infatuated with an Oxford undergraduate, Lord Alfred Douglas, a younger son of the Marquess of Queensberry. Once more he was 'making a fool of himself', but it soon became apparent that the side effects of the relationship on Wilde's personality and conduct were much more corrosive, especially when combined with the money and acclaim from his first real success, the play Lady Windermere's Fan, *which opened in February 1892. The passage from Conan Doyle's memoirs quoted above continues:*

Oscar Wilde and Lord Alfred Douglas, both smoking, in a photograph taken in 1893. Lady Bracknell says on hearing that Jack smokes in The Importance of Being Earnest, *'I am glad to hear it. A man should always have an occupation of some kind. There are far too many idle men in London as it is.'*

Only once again did I see him, many years afterwards, and then he gave me the impression of being mad. He asked me, I remember, if I had seen some play of his which was running. I answered that I had not. He said: 'Ah, you must go. It is wonderful. It is genius!' All this with the gravest face. Nothing could have been more different from his early gentlemanly instincts.

There were plenty of other witnesses to the transformation. In 1893, just before and after the opening of Wilde's second play, A Woman of No Importance, *Max Beerbohm, then an Oxford contemporary of Douglas, wrote a series of letters to his friend Reggie Turner:*

12 April—I am sorry to say that Oscar drinks far more than he ought: indeed the first time I saw him, after all that long period of distant adoration and reverence, he was in a hopeless state of intoxication. He has deteriorated very much in appearance: his cheeks being quite a dark purple and fat to a fault. I think he will die of apoplexy on the first night of the play.

15 April—Did I tell you about Oscar at the restaurant in my last note to you? I think not. During the rehearsal, he went to a place with my brother* to have some lunch. He ordered a watercress sandwich: which in due course was brought to him: not a thin, diaphanous green thing such as he had meant but a very stout, satisfying article of food. This he ate with assumed disgust (but evident relish) and when he paid the waiter, he said 'Tell the cook of this restaurant with the compliments of Mr Oscar Wilde that these are the very worst sandwiches in the whole world and that, when I ask for a watercress sandwich, I do not mean a loaf with a field in the middle of it.'

21 April—Have you read any of the notices of Oscar's play? The first night was very brilliant in its audience . . . Balfour and Chamberlain and all the politicians were there. When little Oscar came on to make his bow there was a slight mingling of hoots and hisses, though he looked very sweet in a new white waistcoat and a large bunch of little lilies in his coat. The notices are better than I had expected: the piece is sure of a long, of a very long run, despite all that the critics may say in its favour.

Last night I went again: the Prince also there. He had command of the Royal Box (is it not the irony of fate?) just after it had been allotted to Mrs Langtry.† I believe she suggested that they should share it but the Prince was adamant. After the play I supped with Oscar and Alfred Douglas (who is staying with him) and my brother at the Albemarle. Oscar told us one lovely thing. A little journalist who had several times attacked him vulgarly came up to him in the street the other day and cordially accosted him. Oscar stared at him and said after a moment or two 'You will pardon me: I remember your name perfectly but I can't recall your face.'

13 May—You need not, by the way, be jealous of Alfred Douglas as he does not peculiarly fascinate me: he is for one thing obviously mad (like all his family I believe).

Wilde's masterpiece, The Importance of Being Earnest, *opened on 14 February 1895. The mad, bullying Lord Queensberry arrived at the theatre with a professional prize-fighter as back-up, intent on causing a scene, but was thwarted and could only leave a bouquet of vegetables. He departed, according to Wilde, 'chattering like a monstrous ape'. This was not the first such incident. Queensberry's eldest son was secretary to Lord Rosebery. In 1893 Queensberry had threatened to horsewhip Rosebery and called him a 'snob queer'. On 28 February Queensberry left a card at Wilde's club with a note on it: 'To Oscar Wilde posing as a somdomite'* [sic]. *E. F. Benson tells what followed his attack on Wilde.*

* Max's half-brother, Herbert Beerbohm Tree, was producing and taking a leading role in the play.
† Lady Warwick had replaced her in the Prince's affections.

Oscar Wilde, by Henri de Toulouse-Lautrec

The whole tragic business sprang from that act of inconceivable folly when (his life having been what it was) he brought a libel action against Lord Queensberry. Then in the witness-box, when being cross-examined by Mr Edward Carson, he made the further deplorable error of being flippant, and though he was both dexterous and witty, this was a ghastly mistake.

For three days the trial lasted, and then the prosecution was withdrawn and the jury gave the verdict in favour of Lord Queensberry as having proved justification for the libel. Other trials followed, for such was the nature of the evidence of which he had made a jest that the Home Office ordered a prosecution against him for indecent offences. At this second trial the jury disagreed, and the Home Office under the direction of Mr H. H. Asquith instituted a third. He had already lost friends, position and reputation, his career, as far as could be foreseen, both as author and playwright, was finished, but the law had to take its course. At that third trial he was convicted, and the judge passed on him the most severe sentence that the law permitted. That probably reflected the bulk of public opinion in England, and a plebiscite would have approved any amount of trials in order to obtain a conviction and the severest sentence possible. The wave of retribution towered and curled over and smashed him; he had been made a scapegoat, and now the wretched animal was dragged ceremoniously off into the salt desert of tribulation.

In 1897, shortly before he left Reading Gaol—the 'salt desert' chosen for him—Wilde completed a very long letter to Alfred Douglas, which came to be known as De Profundis: From the Depths. *It is an extraordinary effusion, both an attempt to bring home to Douglas his part in the tragedy, and also an exposition of the purifying effect which, Wilde claimed, his prison experience had had on him. The first extract recounts Wilde's transfer from Wandsworth to Reading, and then come a series of his broadsides aimed at Douglas, before he turns to the topics of humility and the simple life.*

To each of us different fates are meted out. My lot has been one of public infamy, of long imprisonment, of misery, of ruin, of disgrace, but I am not worthy of it—not yet, at any rate. I remember that I used to say that I thought I could bear a real tragedy if it came to me with purple pall and a mask of noble sorrow, but that the dreadful thing about modernity was that it put tragedy into the raiment of comedy, so that the great realities seemed commonplace or grotesque or lacking in style. It is quite true about modernity. It has probably always been true about actual life. It is said that all martyrdoms seemed mean to the looker on. The nineteenth century is no exception to the rule.

Everything about my tragedy has been hideous, mean, repellent, lacking in style; our very dress makes us grotesque. We are the zanies of sorrow. We are clowns whose hearts are broken. We are specially designed to appeal to the sense of humour. On 13 November 1895, I was brought down here from London. From two o'clock till half-past two on that day I had to stand on the centre platform of Clapham Junction in convict dress, and handcuffed, for the world to look at. I had been taken out of the hospital ward without a moment's notice being given to me. Of all possible objects I was the most grotesque. When people saw me they laughed. Each train as it came up swelled the audience. Nothing could exceed their amusement. That was, of course, before they knew who I was. As soon as they had been informed they laughed still more. For half an hour I stood there in the grey November rain surrounded by a jeering mob.

For a year after that was done to me I wept every day at the same hour and for the same space of time. That is not such a tragic thing as possibly it sounds to you. To those who are in prison tears are a part of every day's experience. A day in prison on which one does not weep is a day on which one's heart is hard, not a day on which one's heart is happy.

I am not speaking in phrases of rhetorical exaggeration but in terms of absolute truth to actual fact when I remind you that during the whole time we were together I never wrote one single line. In September '93, I arrived at St James's Place every morning at half-past eleven, in order to have the opportunity of thinking and writing without the interruptions inseparable from my own household [in Tite Street, Chelsea], quiet and peaceful as that household was. But the attempt was vain. At twelve o'clock you drove up, and stayed smoking cigarettes and chattering till half-past one, when I had to take you out to luncheon at the Café Royal or the Berkeley. Luncheon with its liqueurs lasted usually till half-past three. For an hour you retired to White's. At tea-time you appeared again, and stayed till it was time to dress for dinner. You dined with me either at the Savoy or at Tite Street. We did not separate as a rule till after midnight, as supper at Willis's had to wind up the entrancing day. That was my life for those three months, every single day, except during the four days when you went abroad. I then, of course, had to go over to Calais to fetch you back. For one of my nature and temperament it was a position at once grotesque and tragic.

You surely must realise that now? You must see now that your incapacity of being alone: your nature so exigent in its persistent claim on the attention and time of others: your lack of any power of sustained intellectual concentration: the unfortunate accident—for I like to think it was no more—that you had not yet been able to acquire the 'Oxford temper' in intellectual matters, never, I mean, been one who could play gracefully with ideas but had arrived at violence of opinion merely—that all these things, combined with the fact that your desires and interests were in Life not in Art, were as destructive to your own progress in culture as they were to my work as an artist?

While you were with me you were the absolute ruin of my Art, and in allowing you to stand persistently between Art and myself I give to myself shame and blame in the fullest degree. You couldn't know, you couldn't understand, you couldn't appreciate. I had no right to expect it of you at all. Your interests were merely in your meals and moods. Your desires were simply for amusements, for ordinary or less ordinary pleasures. They were what your temperament needed, or thought it needed for the moment. I should have forbidden you my house and my chambers except when I specially invited you. I blame myself without reserve for my weakness.

I let myself be lured into long spells of senseless and sensual ease. I amused myself with being a *flâneur*, a dandy, a man of fashion. I surrounded myself with the smaller natures and the meaner minds. I became the spendthrift of my own genius, and to waste an eternal youth gave me a curious joy. Tired of being on the heights I deliberately went to the depths in the search for new sensations. What the paradox was to me in the sphere of thought, perversity became to me in the sphere of passion. Desire, at the end, was a malady, or a madness, or both. I grew careless of the lives of others. I took pleasure where it pleased me and passed on. I forgot that every little action of the common day makes or unmakes character, and that therefore what one has done in the secret chamber one has some day to cry aloud on the housetops. I ceased to be Lord over myself. I was no longer the Captain of my Soul, and did not know it. I allowed you to dominate me, and your father to frighten me. I ended in horrible disgrace. There is only one thing for me now, absolute humility: just as there is only one thing for you, absolute humility also. You had better come down into the dust and learn it beside me.

I have a strange longing for the great simple primeval things, such as the Sea, to me no less of a mother than the Earth. It seems to me that we all look at Nature too much, and live with her too little. I discern great sanity in the Greek attitude. They never chattered about sunsets, or discussed whether the shadows on the grass were really mauve or not. But they saw that the sea was for the swimmer, and the sand for the feet of the runner. They loved the trees for the shadow that they cast, and the forest for its silence at noon. The vineyard-dresser wreathed his hair with ivy that he might keep off the rays of the sun as he stooped over the young shoots, and for the artist and the athlete, the two types that Greece gave us, they plaited into garlands the leaves of the bitter laurel and of the wild parsley which else had been of no service to man.

We call ourselves a utilitarian age, and we do not know the uses of any single thing. We have forgotten that Water can cleanse, and Fire purify, and that the Earth is mother to us all. As a consequence our Art is of the Moon and plays with shadows, while Greek art is of the Sun and deals directly with things. I feel sure that in elemental forces there is purification, and I want to go back to them and live in their presence. Of course, to one so modern as I am, *enfant de mon siècle*, merely to look at the world will be always lovely. I tremble with pleasure when I think that on the very day of my leaving prison both the laburnum and the lilac will be blooming in the gardens, and that I shall see the wind stir into restless beauty the swaying gold of the one, and make the other toss the pale purple of its plumes so that all the air shall be Arabia for me. Society, as we have constituted it, will have no place for me, has none to offer; but Nature, whose sweet rains fall on unjust and just alike, will have clefts in the rocks where I may hide, and secret valleys in whose silence I may weep undisturbed. She will hang the night with stars so that I may walk abroad in the darkness without stumbling, and send the wind over my footprints so that none may track me to my hurt: she will cleanse me in great waters, and with bitter herbs make me whole.

When a shortened and bowdlerised version of De Profundis *was published in 1905, Max Beerbohm quickly exposed Wilde's change of heart for what it was.*

'There is only one thing left for me now,' he writes, 'absolute humility.' And about humility he writes many beautiful and true things. And, doubtless, while he wrote them, he had the sensation of humility. Humble he was not. Emotion was not seeking outlet: emotion came through its own expression. The artist spoke, and the man obeyed. The attitude was struck, and the heart pulsated to it. Perhaps a Cardinal Archbishop, when he kneels to wash the feet of the beggars, is filled with humility, and revels in the experience. Such was Oscar Wilde's humility. It was the luxurious complement of pride ... In prison Oscar Wilde was still himself—still with the same artistry in words, still with the same detachment from life. We see him here as the spectator of his own tragedy. His tragedy was great. It is one of the tragedies that will live always in romantic history. And the protagonist had an artist's joy in it.

Beerbohm's judgement is borne out by the tone of remarks made by Wilde, even before he was back in the swim. In April 1897 when writing to his friend Robbie Ross about duplicating the manuscript of De Profundis, *he said, 'I assure you that the typewriting machine, when played with expression, is no more annoying than the piano when played by a sister or near relation.' In May, when greeted by the novelist Ada Leverson on his final release from gaol, he riposted, 'How marvellous of you to know exactly the right hat to wear at seven o'clock in the morning to meet a friend who has been away!' By August he had seen 'Bosie' Douglas again in France, and in September went to live with him in Naples, while freely admitting that Bosie was 'a gilded pillar of infamy'. To Reggie Turner he said, 'He ruined my life, and for that very reason I seem forced to love him more: and I think now I shall do lovely work.' But by then he had already completed his last masterpiece, 'The Ballad of Reading Gaol', inspired by memories of the execution of Charles Thomas Wooldridge in Reading Gaol in July 1896, for murdering his wife. He was quite right when he said in October 1897, 'I think bits of the poem very good now, but I will never again out-Kipling Henley.'* *

He walked amongst the Trial Men
    In a suit of shabby grey;
A cricket cap was on his head,
    And his step seemed light and gay;
But I never saw a man who looked
    So wistfully at the day.

I never saw a man who looked
    With such a wistful eye
Upon that little tent of blue
    Which prisoners call the sky,
And at every drifting cloud that went
    With sails of silver by.

I walked, with other souls in pain,
    Within another ring,
And was wondering if the man had done
    A great or little thing,
When a voice behind me whispered low,
    'That fellow's got to swing.'

* Rudyard Kipling and W. E. Henley were two, very full-blooded, exponents of the ballad form at the time.

Lord Wolseley; only the pince-nez slightly detracts from his martial air

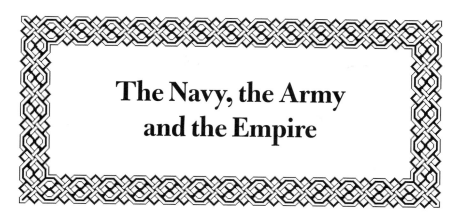

The Navy, the Army
and the Empire

Britain's first line of defence had always been her Navy rather than her Army, and her newly acquired and far-flung Empire seemed only to emphasise this order of priorities. At the time of the Diamond Jubilee in 1897 a loyal versifier from Cape Breton in Nova Scotia summoned up a vivid image of the vast sea spaces to be traversed:

Here's to Queen Victoria
Dressed in all her regalia
With one foot in Canada
And the other in Australia

In 1895 Lord Wolseley, the original of Gilbert and Sullivan's Modern Major-General, was appointed Commander-in-Chief in succession to the Queen's unimaginative and deeply conservative cousin, the Duke of Cambridge, who had been fifty-eight years in the Army, thirty-nine of them as Commander-in-Chief. Even Wolseley had no doubts as to which was the Senior Service, reminding his wife that 'I have said in a public speech — more than once, I think — that if we had only one million to spend on defences, I would spend it on our Navy, our first, our only great line of defence.' In 1887 Lord Ronald Gower had seen the fleet assembled for the Golden Jubilee Review at Spithead: 'a wonderful display of ironclads and crafts of all kinds . . . at least one hundred millions were represented on these waters.' In the evening, after 'the Royal Yacht had steamed slowly through the long lines of battleships . . . there was a display of rockets such as, I suppose, was never seen at sea before . . . The proceedings ended by a fine display of the electric searchlight.' In spite of the impression given by this Review there were concerns about the real state of the Navy, fuelled by inside information fed to the Press by 'Jackie' Fisher, the future First Sea Lord. These led to the Naval Defence Act of 1889 which incorporated a building programme for seventy new ships costing £21.5 million over five years. It was at this moment that the hierarchy of battleships, cruisers for worldwide trade protection, and torpedo boat 'catchers' or 'destroyers' was established.

Unfortunately, the British enthusiasm for things naval was shared by the Kaiser, who had ample opportunity to observe what was going on during his annual visits to his grandmother for the Cowes Regatta, which of course took place opposite Britain's biggest naval base at Portsmouth. Germany might have missed out in the scramble for colonies but as the Kaiser's mother, the Empress Frederick, reported to her own mother, Queen Victoria, in 1894, 'William's one idea is to have a navy which shall be larger and stronger than the British navy.' At the Diamond Jubilee Spithead Review, twenty-one battleships, fifty-three cruisers, thirty destroyers, and twenty-four torpedo boats were assembled—but these were just from home commands round Britain. The naval estimates stood at £22 million, double those for 1884. Rudyard Kipling is normally associated with the Army, particularly in India, but shortly after the 1897 Review he went out on exercise with the Channel Fleet. He had a deep love affair with technology and delighted in the close proximity which he could have to all the latest tools of destruction—a delight which can be seen in the following extracts from the book A Fleet in Being, *which he wrote about the trip. But, being Kipling, he also recorded the moment when 'the horror of the thing' dawned on him.*

We, of the Northern Squadron, found Lough Swilly in full possession of a sou'-west gale, and an assortment of dingy colliers lying where they could most annoy the anchoring Fleet. A collier came alongside with donkey-engines that would not lift more than half their proper load; she had no bags, no shovels, and her crazy derrick-boom could not be topped up enough to let the load clear our bulwarks. So we supplied our own bags and shovels, rearranged the boom, put two of our own men on the rickety donkey-engines, and fell to work in that howling wind and wet.

As a preparation for war next day, it seemed a little hard on the crew, who worked like sailors—there is no stronger term. From time to time a red-eyed black demon, with flashing teeth, shot into the ward-room for a bite and a drink, cried out the number of tons aboard, added a few pious words on the collier's appliances, and our bunkers, and tore back to where the donkey-engines wheezed, the bags crashed, the shovels rasped and scraped, the boom whined and creaked, and the First Lieutenant, carved in pure jet, said precisely what occurred to him.

Descend by the slippery steel ladders into the bluish copper-smelling

*The Diamond
Jubilee Naval
Review at Spithead
by C. Dixon*

haze of hurrying mechanism all crowded under the protective deck; crawl along the greasy foot-plates, and stand with your back against the lengthwise bulkhead that separates the desperately whirling twin engines. Wait under the low-browed supporting-columns till the roar and the quiver has soaked into every nerve of you; till your knees loosen and your heart begins to pump. Feel the floors lift below you to the jar and batter of the defrauded propeller as it draws out of its element. Try now to read the dizzying gauge-needles or find a meaning in the rumbled signals from the bridge. Creep into the stoke-hold—a boiler blistering either ear as you stoop—and taste what tinned air is like for a while.

No description will make you realise the almost infernal mobility of a Fleet at sea. I had seen ours called, to all appearance, out of the deep; split in twain at a word, and, at a word, sent skimming beyond the horizon; strung out as vultures string out patiently in the hot sky above a dying beast; flung like a lasso; gathered anew as a riata [lariat] is coiled at the saddle bow; dealt out card-fashion over fifty miles of green table; picked up, shuffled, and redealt as the game changed. I had seen cruisers flown like hawks, ridden like horses at a close finish, and manoeuvred like bicycles; but the wonder of their appearance and disappearance never failed. The *Powerful* spoke, and in ten minutes the cruiser-squadron had vanished; each ship taking her own matches and sulphur to make a hell of her own. And what that hell might be if worked at full power I could, presently, guess as we swung round a headland, and the bugles began. At this point the gunner became a person of importance (in the Navy each hour of the day has its king), and the captains of the guns separated themselves a little from the common herd. Remember,

177

we were merely a third-class cruiser, capable, perhaps, of slaying destroyers in a heavy sea, but meant for the most part to scout and observe. Our armament consisted of eight four-inch quick-fire wire guns, the newest type—two on the foc'sle, four in the waist, and two on the poop, alternating with as many three-pounder Hotchkiss quick-firers. Three Maxims adorned the low nettings. Their water-jackets were filled up from an innocent tin-pot before the game began. It looked like slaking the thirst of devils.

We found an eligible rock, the tip of a greyish headland, peopled by a few gulls—the surge creaming along its base—and a portion of this we made our target, that we might see the effect of the shots and practise the men at firing on a water-line. Up came the beautiful solid brass cordite cartridges; and the four-inch shells that weigh twenty-five pounds apiece. (The little three-pounders, as you know, have their venomous shell and charge together like small-arm ammunition.) The filled belts of the Maxims were adjusted, and all these man-slaying devilries waked to life and peered over the side at the unsuspecting gulls. It was 'still' throughout the ship—still as it will be when the Real Thing arrives. From the upper bridge I could hear, above the beat of the engines, the click of the lieutenants' scabbards (*Why* should men who need every freedom in action be hampered by an utterly useless sword?); the faint clink of a four-inch breech swung open; the crisper snick of the little Hotchkiss's falling-block; and an impatient sewing-machine noise from a Maxim making sure of its lock-action. On his platform over my head the Navigating Officer was giving the ranges to the rock.

'Two thousand seven hundred yards, sir.'

'Two thousand seven hundred yards'—the order passed from gun to gun—'ten knots right deflection—starboard battery.' The gun-captains muzzled the rubber-faced shoulder-pieces, and the long lean muzzles behind the shields shifted fractionally.

'Try a sighting shot with that three-pounder!'

The smack of cordite is keener, and catches one more about the heart, than the slower-burning black powder. There was a shrillish gasping wail—exactly like the preliminary whoop of an hysterical woman—as the little shell hurried to the target; and a puff of dirty smoke on the rock-face sent the gulls flying. So far as I could observe there was not even a haze round the lips of the gun. Till I saw the spent case jerked out I did not know which of the clean, precise, and devilish four had spoken.

'Two thousand four hundred,' the voice droned overhead, and the starboard bow four-inch quick-firer opened the ball. Again no smoke; again the song of the shell—not a shriek this time, but a most utterly mournful wail. Again the few seconds' suspense (what will they be when

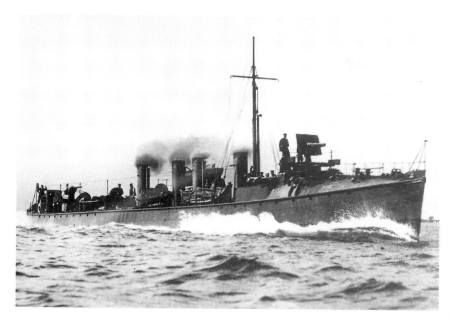

HMS Hornet,
*Admiral Fisher's
first torpedo boat
destroyer*

the Real Thing comes?) and a white star on the target. The cruiser winced a little, as though someone had pinched her.

Before the next gun had fired, the empty cartridge cylinder of the first was extracted, and by some sleight of hand I could not see the breech had closed behind a full charge. A Martini-Henri could hardly have been reloaded more swiftly.

'Two thousand three hundred,' cried the reader of that day's lessons, and we fell seriously to work; high shriek and low wail following in an infernal fugue, through which, with no regard for decency, the Maxims quacked and jabbered insanely. The rock was splintered and ripped and gashed in every direction, and great pieces of it bounded into the sea.

'Two thousand one hundred.'

'Good shot. Oh, good shot! That was a water-liner . . . That was the Marines' three-pounder. Good! . . . Ah—ah! Bad. Damn bad! Short! Miles short! Who fired that shot?'

A shell had burst short of the mark, and the captain of that gun was asked politely if he supposed Government supplied him with three-pound shell for the purpose of shooting mackerel.

And so we went on, till the big guns had fired their quota and the Maxims ran out in one last fiends' flurry, and target-practice for the month was over. The rock that had been grey was white, and a few shining cartridge-cases lay beside each gun.

Then the horror of the thing began to soak into me. What I had seen was a slow peddling-out of Admiralty allowance for the month, and it seemed to me more like squirting death through a hose than any ordinary gun-practice. What will it be when all the ammunition-hoists are working, when the Maxims' water-jacket puffs off in steam; when the three-pounder charges come up a dozen at a time to be spent twenty to the minute; when the sole limit of four-inch fire is the speed with which the shells and cases can be handled? What will it be when the Real Thing is upon us?

Home we cruisers all went to Portland, past the Wolf and the toothed edges of the Scillies, astonishing the crowded Channel traffic—sometimes a Jersey potato-ketch full of curiosity; or a full-rigged trader of the deep sea, bound for one or other of the Capes; a Norwegian, Dane, German, or Frenchman; and now and again a white-sided, brass bejewelled yacht. That was a Royal progress. No blind man's buff off the Lizard or dreary game of hunt-the-Needles such as the liners play, but through the heavenly clear night the leisurely, rolling slow-march of the overlords of all the seas.

And the whole thing was my very own (that is to say yours); mine to me by right of birth. Mine were the speed and power of the hulls, not here only but the world over; the hearts and brains and lives of the trained men; such strength and such power as we and the world dare hardly guess at. And holding this power in the hollow of my hand; able at the word to exploit the earth to my own advantage; to gather me treasure and honour, as men reckon honour, I (and a few million friends of mine) forbore because we were white men. Any other breed with this engine at their disposal would have used it savagely long ago. Thus I stood, astounded at my own moderation, and counted up my possessions with most sinful pride.

The wind, and the smell of it off the coasts, was mine, and it was telling me things it would never dream of confiding to a foreigner. The short, hollow Channel sea was mine—bought for me drop by drop, every salt drop of it, in the last eight hundred years—as short a time as it takes to make a perfect lawn in a cathedral close. The speech on the deck below was mine, for the men were free white men, same as me, only considerably better. Their notions of things were my notions of things, and the bulk of those notions we could convey one to the other without opening our heads.

We had a common tradition, one thousand years old, of the things one takes for granted. A warrant officer said something, and the groups melted quietly about some job or other. That same caste of man—that same type of voice—was speaking in the commissariat in Burma; in barracks in Rangoon; under double awnings in the Persian Gulf; on the

Rock at Gibraltar—wherever else you please—and the same instant obedience, I knew, would follow on that voice. And a foreigner would never have understood—will never understand!

Rudyard Kipling by Philip Burne-Jones, son of Edward

Victoria may have been Queen of the United Kingdom, but she was Empress of India. Tens of thousands of Britons experienced life there, as ordinary soldiers, or merchants, planters, or administrators. Lady

Wilson was a perceptive Scotswoman, born Ann Macleod in 1855, who married a senior member of the Indian Civil Service in 1888 and went out to make a life there. She first describes the 'colossal administration' of the Raj:

Our dak bungalow* gives us an opportunity to receive many a welcome guest. You may well ask what brings these stray visitors here? It is all the result of a huge system of inspection in every section of the vast machinery of Government, to ensure that every worker, whether English or Indian, is doing his work satisfactorily, so that the colossal administration may run smoothly.

It is an important moment when an inspector appears on the horizon, with blessings or curses on his wings, for on the result of his inspection and approval or disapproval of the work accomplished hangs censure or promotion. The Deputy Inspector-General of Police appears, and the men turn out for the inspection of their arms, uniform and accoutrements, and of their proficiency in drill. The Civil Surgeon arrives in an outlying dispensary and sees that the instruments are clean, that the supply of medicine is sufficient, that poisons are safely under lock and key, that prescriptions have been suitably chosen for the different cases, and that the patients in hospital are well cared for and comfortable. The Executive Engineer satisfies himself that the roads, bridges, and public buildings have been properly repaired; the Canal Engineer examines the condition of the channels and masonry-work required for the precious water which fertilises the miles of fields. Finally, the Deputy Commissioner and his superior, the Commissioner of the Division, separately inspect again everything which has already been inspected, listen to any complaints, and do their best to rectify all grievances.

So they flit across the stage and disappear, Railway Inspectors, School Inspectors, Land Revenue, Jail, Forest, Geological, Mineralogical, and every other logical Inspector, all links in the mighty chain which connects the watchman of the smallest village with the Secretary of State for India, and an Empress with her greatest dependency. Every head of all the districts that form the squares upon this mighty chessboard meets the other pieces in the great game, benefits from their expert advice, and does what he can to speed them on their way.

Whatever her love for them, Lady Wilson saw the difficulty, if not impossibility, of understanding the Indians, and how this was exacerbated by the 'good form' instilled into the Britons who ran the subcontinent by their public school education.

* Guest quarters for official visitors.

A Peep at the Train, by Rudolph Swoboda, an artist commissioned by Queen Victoria to go out to India to paint a series of portraits of her subjects there

Think of us in a great tract of country covering three thousand square miles, studded with towns and villages, and holding half a million human beings, for whose well-being Jim [her husband] is responsible. Realise that a thousand men work under him, all of whom, with the exception of the doctor, civil engineer, policeman, and assistant commissioner, are Indian. Then add to that undying curiosity about the whole of them, and judge if monotony is possible for an hour!

I love them all in an unreasoning blind way. The look of their brown villages perched on little hills and built on the ruins of dead homes, has its own note of greeting. The very smell of the village smoke, by which one knows in the dark that these old homesteads are near, is dear to me, and brings with it the sense of elemental things. I love to watch the big clumsy bullocks, driven by a child, lazily swinging back in the gloaming from the wells they have worked in the heat of the day, or the ploughs they have dragged over dusty fields, sure of a place in the family court-yard and a well-earned meal from their faithful friends. Just at this hour, so one dreams, this has happened for centuries. So the cattle will return to their home in the twilight centuries hence. Time and change, with the restless woe they bring in their train, do not surely exist in this land of habit and mute resignation.

The wife of the headman of the village is seated on the ground before a butcher's shop, a bit of goat's flesh on a broad leaf darkened by flies on her lap, while she haggles with the butcher over what the price of the meat should be, and tries to get it for one farthing less than the day's market-rate. In the next shop a shoemaker is bending over a pair of crimson-leather slippers which he is embroidering, unaided by any pattern, with coloured thread. They are surely destined for a bride, and will probably spell debt to her father. The next shop anticipates the sequel. It is a grain-merchant's shop. The low wooden counter is heaped up with bright yellow maize, ochre-brown oil-seed and green peas. On the board above the shop the gods of the Hindu pantheon are painted in bright colours, with a sign in red ochre beneath them, which should bring good luck.

The Hindu grain-merchants are also usurers. These money-lenders are often honest men, but equally often they are not. With their quick brains they learn from the village schoolmaster, at a very early age, how to read and write and cast up accounts, and then they hold the illiterate Muhammadan peasant in the hollow of their hands, for his only knowledge is of the plough which he has followed since he was a child. A wedding and a funeral are the two occasions for feasting which an Indian peasant has in his life, and they are pitfalls for debt which may end in the loss of his lands. A big clumsy farmer seated before the grain-merchant's

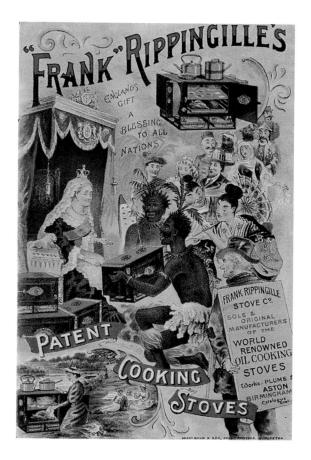

The Queen's image enlisted to help spread the informal empire of commerce

shop is evidently in a tight corner. He is arguing, with a puzzled and angry expression, with the Hindu money-lender, who holds a bit of paper covered with figures in his supple hands. It is probably the old story. The interest of the debt has been paid in cattle, cotton or grain. The Hindu has reckoned these at much less than their market-price. The debt, with the interest due, is bigger than ever. There is only one end to the argument. Threatened and bamboozled, the farmer has at last added his thumbmark to the account as it stands, and accepted all that it involves.

The street is crowded. Men are carrying their little sons on their shoulders, dressed for the occasion in tinsel coat and skull-cap, and eating sugar-cane. Women chatter to one another as they wait for the scones an old hag is baking for them in an oven. There is a jingle of sounds, the clang of the blacksmith's anvil, the wheeze of the bellows which keep up his fire, the tinkle of the bell which the sweetmeat-seller rings behind his gay stall. A wild-looking fakir, stupefied by bhang [cannabis], with matted locks, powdered face, and a long iron staff, repeats the name of his particular god with rapid insistence, and is given alms by his followers. A village postman, with bells attached to a stick, rushes past on his way to some outlying homestead.

The Royal Horse Artillery on Stables Parade in 1888, by G. D. Giles

To me the sounds and the stir of the living panorama are a never-ending delight. And yet I know it is only at the framework of this life I am looking, and I have a sad feeling that themselves I shall never understand; that as far as the East is from the West, so far are we removed from one another.

What impresses me most perhaps, in our talks about everyday life, is the tyranny of public school 'form'. It is not more characteristic of soldiers than of civilians or any typical Englishman. 'The trail of the serpent is over them all,' and they go through their short spells of life with their tall hats as the armorial shield of 'good form' held carefully over their hearts.

An Indian said to me once, 'If the Sahibs would only talk to us about themselves. We are a sentimental people. We could be so easily influenced, if they would only tell us what they think and feel, and let us understand their ideal.' 'That they will never do,' I assured him. 'You may guess what they think by what you see them do. They will work for you and die for you, and if you were to cut them up, you would certainly find India written on their hearts. But they won't talk about it, and if they were more emotional and did, they would have different natures and lose something by the exchange.'

One sees the same thing in the Army. They would die for their country or regiment and long for a chance to prove it, but it is not 'good form' to say so, or to talk apparently about anything when they are together except polo, polo ponies, dogs and sport. They must all be of the same pattern, and woe betide them if they have a hobby of their own, outside of the regimental routine. I sometimes wonder if it is not just this tradi-

186

tional 'form' and its code, the only certainty that a boy carries away with him from his years at a public school, which will land him successfully at the North Pole or help him to rule the inhabitants of the Equator.

Soldiers of the Queen: British tommies in India

After passing out of Sandhurst, Winston Churchill went out with his regiment to Bangalore in southern India. His account of garrison life there, revolving round polo, tends to confirm Lady Wilson's remarks about army officers.

The British lines or cantonments are in accordance with invariable practice placed five or six miles from the populous cities which they guard; and in the intervening space lie the lines of the Indian regiments. The British troops are housed in large, cool, colonnaded barracks. Here forethought and order have been denied neither time nor space in the laying out of their plans. Splendid roads, endless double avenues of shady trees, abundant supplies of pure water; imposing offices, hospitals and institutions; ample parade-grounds and riding-schools characterise these centres of the collective life of considerable white communities.

The climate of Bangalore, at more than three thousand feet above sea level, is excellent. Although the sun strikes with torrid power, the nights except in the hottest months are cool and fresh. The roses of Europe in innumerable large pots attain the highest perfection of fragrance and colour. Flowers, flowering shrubs and creepers blossom in glorious profusion. Snipe (and snakes) abound in the marshes; brilliant butterflies dance in the sunshine, and nautch-girls* by the light of the moon.

No quarters are provided for the officers. They draw instead a lodging allowance which together with their pay and other incidentals fills each month with silver rupees a string net bag as big as a prize turnip. All around the cavalry mess lies a suburb of roomy one-storeyed bungalows standing in their own walled grounds and gardens. The subaltern receives his bag of silver at the end of each month of duty, canters home with it to his bungalow, throws it to his beaming butler, and then in theory has no further material cares. [Churchill shared with two others.] We paid an equal contribution into the pot; and thus freed from mundane cares, devoted ourselves to the serious purpose of life. This was expressed in one word—polo.

I must not forget to say that there were of course also a great many military duties. Just before dawn, every morning, one was awakened by a dusky figure with a clammy hand adroitly lifting one's chin and applying a gleaming razor to a lathered and defenceless throat. By six o'clock the regiment was on parade, and we rode to a wide plain and there drilled and manoeuvred for an hour and a half. We then returned to baths at the bungalow and breakfast in the mess. Then at nine stables and orderly room till about half-past ten; then home to the bungalow before the sun attained its fiercest ray. All the distances in the spread-out cantonment were so great that walking was impossible. We cantered on hacks from one place to another. But the noonday sun asserted his tyrannical authority, and long before eleven o'clock all white men were in shelter. We nipped across to luncheon at half-past one in blistering heat and then returned to sleep till five o'clock. Now the station begins to live again. It is the hour of polo. It is the hour for which we have been living all day long. I was accustomed in those days to play every chukka I could get into [and] very rarely played less than eight and more often ten or twelve.

As the shadows lengthened over the polo ground, we ambled back perspiring and exhausted to hot baths, rest, and at half-past eight dinner, to the strains of the regimental band and the clinking of ice in well-filled glasses. Thereafter those who were not so unlucky as to be caught by the senior officers to play a tiresome game then in vogue called 'whist', sat smoking in the moonlight till half-past ten or eleven at the latest signalled the 'And so to bed'. Such was 'the long, long Indian day' as I knew it for three years; and not such a bad day either.

Churchill was then able to use his powerful connections in London to get
* Indian dancing-girls.

himself seconded to a punitive expedition on the North-West Frontier of India. There he saw action for the first time when, one morning, he found himself a member of a small detachment from the main brigade.

I lay down with an officer and eight Sikhs on the side of the village towards the mountain, while the remainder of the company rummaged about the mud houses or sat down and rested behind them. A quarter of an hour passed and nothing happened. Then the captain of the company arrived.

'We are going to withdraw,' he said to the subaltern. 'You stay here and cover our retirement till we take up a fresh position on that knoll below the village.' He added, 'The Buffs* don't seem to be coming up, and the colonel thinks we are rather in the air here.'

It struck me this was a sound observation. We waited another ten minutes. Meanwhile I presumed, for I could not see them, the main body of the company was retiring from the village towards the lower knoll. Suddenly the mountainside sprang to life. Swords flashed from behind rocks, bright flags waved here and there. A dozen widely-scattered white smoke-puffs broke from the rugged face in front of us. Loud explosions resounded close at hand. From high up on the crag, one thousand, two thousand, three thousand feet above us, white or blue figures appeared, dropping down the mountainside from ledge to ledge like monkeys down the branches of a tall tree. A shrill crying arose from many points. Yi! Yi! Yi! Bang! Bang! Bang! The whole hillside began to be spotted with smoke, and tiny figures descended every moment nearer towards us. Our eight Sikhs opened an independent fire, which soon became more and more rapid. The hostile figures continued to flow down the mountainside, and scores began to gather in rocks about a hundred yards away from us. The targets were too tempting to be resisted. I borrowed the Martini of the Sikh by whom I lay. He was quite content to hand me cartridges. I began to shoot carefully at the men gathering in the rocks. A lot of bullets whistled about us. But we lay very flat, and no harm was done. This lasted perhaps five minutes in continuous crescendo. We had certainly found the adventure for which we had been looking. Then an English voice close behind. It was the battalion adjutant.

'Come on back now. There is no time to lose. We can cover you from the knoll.'

The Sikh whose rifle I had borrowed had put eight or ten cartridges on the ground beside me. It was a standing rule to let no ammunition fall into the hands of the tribesmen. The Sikh seemed rather excited, so I handed him the cartridges one after the other to put in his pouch. This

* The East Kent Regiment.

189

Pathan tribesmen ambushing British troops on the North-West Frontier of India; engraving after Vereker Hamilton

was a lucky inspiration. The rest of our party got up and turned to retreat. There was a ragged volley from the rocks; shouts, exclamations, and a scream. I thought for the moment that five or six of our men had lain down again. So they had: two killed and three wounded. One man was shot through the breast and pouring with blood; another lay on his back kicking and twisting. The British officer was spinning round just behind me, his face a mass of blood, his right eye cut out. Yes, it was certainly an adventure.

It is a point of honour on the Indian frontier not to leave wounded men behind. Death by inches and hideous mutilation are the invariable measure meted out to all who fall in battle into the hands of the Pathan tribesmen. Back came the adjutant, with another British officer of subaltern rank, a Sikh sergeant-major, and two or three soldiers. We all laid hands on the wounded and began to carry and drag them away down the hill. We got through the few houses, ten or twelve men carrying four, and emerged upon a bare strip of ground. Here stood the captain commanding the company with half-a-dozen men. Beyond and below, one hundred and fifty yards away, was the knoll on which a supporting party should have been posted. No sign of them! Perhaps it was the knoll lower down. We hustled the wounded along, regardless of their protests. We had no rearguard of any kind. All were carrying the wounded. I was therefore sure that worse was close at our heels. We were not half-way across the open space when twenty or thirty furious figures appeared among the houses, firing frantically or waving their swords.

I could only follow by fragments what happened after that. One of the two Sikhs helping to carry my wounded man was shot through the calf. He shouted with pain; his turban fell off; and his long black hair streamed over his shoulders—a tragic golliwog. Two more men came from below and seized hold of our man. The new subaltern and I got the golliwog by the collar and dragged him along the ground. Luckily it was all down hill. Apparently we hurt him so much on the sharp rocks that he asked to be let go alone. He hopped and crawled and staggered and stumbled, but made a good pace. Thus he escaped. I looked round to my left. The adjutant had been shot. Four of his soldiers were carrying him. He was a heavy man, and they all clutched at him. Out from the edge of the houses rushed half a dozen Pathan swordsmen. The bearers of the poor adjutant let him fall and fled at their approach. The leading tribesman rushed upon the prostrate figure and slashed it three or four times with his sword. I forgot everything else at this moment except a desire to kill this man. I wore my long cavalry sword well sharpened. After all, I had won the public schools fencing medal. I resolved on personal combat *à l'arme blanche*. The savage saw me coming. I was not more than twenty yards away. He picked up a big stone and hurled it at me with his left hand, and then awaited me, brandishing his sword. There were others waiting not far behind him. I changed my mind about the cold steel. I pulled out my revolver, took, as I thought, most careful aim, and fired. No result. I fired again. No result. I fired again. Whether I hit him or not I cannot tell. At any rate he ran back two or three yards and plumped down behind a rock. The fusillade was continuous. I looked around. I was all alone with the enemy. Not a friend was to be seen. I ran as fast as I could. There were bullets everywhere. I got to the first knoll. Hurrah, there were the Sikhs holding the lower one! They made vehement gestures, and in a few moments I was among them.

There was still about three-quarters of a mile of the spur to traverse before the plain was reached, and on each side of us other spurs ran downwards. Along these rushed our pursuers, striving to cut us off and firing into both our flanks. I don't know how long we took to get to the bottom. But it was all done quite slowly and steadfastly. We carried two wounded officers and about six wounded Sikhs with us. That took about twenty men. We left one officer and a dozen men dead and wounded to be cut to pieces on the spur.

During this business I armed myself with the Martini and ammunition of a dead man, and fired as carefully as possible thirty or forty shots at tribesmen on the left-hand ridge at distances from eighty to a hundred and twenty yards. The difficulty about these occasions is that one is so out of breath and quivering with exertion, if not with excitement. However, I am sure I never fired without taking aim. We fetched up at the bottom of the spur little better than a mob, but still with our wounded. There was the company reserve and the lieutenant-colonel commanding the battalion and a few orderlies. [The tribesmen were kept at bay until the Buffs arrived.]

There was as much, if not more, attention focused on Egypt and the African Continent, as on India, during these years. In the early 1880s there had been two major blows to British prestige. In 1881 the Transvaal Boers had routed a British force at Majuba Hill and so regained their independence. Although nominally ruled by the Khedive, Egypt had in fact been administered by Britain since Wolseley defeated an uprising there at the Battle of Tel-el-Kebir in 1882. In 1885 Wolseley's relief expedition was too late to stop General Charles Gordon being killed in the Sudan, then seen as a dependency of Egypt, by the fundamentalist Muslim leader known as the Mahdi. The fact that Gordon was killed because he chose to ignore his instructions was forgotten in the general outcry, led by the Queen. Two years earlier one of Gordon's lieutenants, the Austrian-born Rudolf von Slatin, had been imprisoned by the Mahdi, in spite of having converted to Islam. He was held prisoner until he escaped in 1895, ten years after Gordon's severed head had been brought for him to see. He published a best seller in 1896, Fire and Sword in the Sudan, *read avidly by the Queen. Here he recounts the first stage of his escape from Omdurman.*

It was three hours after sunset. We had offered the evening prayer with the Khalifa [the Mahdi's successor], and he had withdrawn to his apartment. Another hour passed without interruption. My lord and master had retired to rest. I rose, took the *farwa* (the rug on which we pray) and the *farda* (a light woollen cloth for protection against the cold) on my shoulders, and went across the mosque to the road that leads north. I heard a low cough, the signal of Muhammad, the intermediary in my escape, and I stood still. He had brought a donkey. I mounted, and was off. The night was dark. The cold, northerly wind had driven the people into their huts and houses. Without meeting a soul we reached the end of the town where a small ruined house stands obliquely to the road, from which a man led out a saddled camel. 'This is your guide. His name is Zeki Belal,' said Muhammad. 'He will guide you to the riding camels that are waiting concealed in the desert. Make haste. A happy journey, and God protect you.'

The man sprang into the saddle, and I got up and sat behind him.

A jingoistic sheet music cover produced after the Bombardment of Alexandria and Battle of Tel-el-Kebir

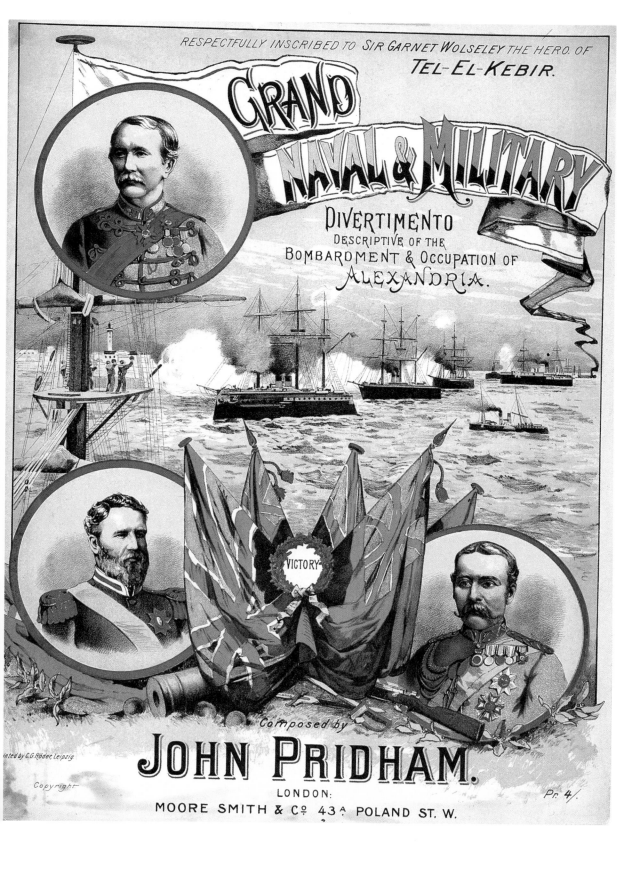

Highland soldiers visit the Sphinx after their victorious Egyptian campaign in 1882

After about an hour's ride, we arrived at the spot where the camels were hidden among some low trees. All was ready, and I mounted the animal assigned to me.

'Zeki,' said I, 'did Muhammad give you the medicine?'

'No; what medicine?'

'They call them ether pills. They keep off sleep and strengthen you on the journey.'

He laughed. 'Sleep!' said he. 'Have no fear on that account. Fear is the child of good folk, and will keep sleep from our eyes, and God in his mercy will fortify us.' The man was right enough. We rode in a northerly direction. The halfa grass and the mimosa trees, which in places grew rather close together, prevented the camels from making rapid progress in the darkness. At sunrise we reached Wadi Bishara, a valley extending here to a breadth of about three miles, which is sown in the rainy season with millet by the Jaalin tribes who live along the Nile.

We drove the creatures at their swiftest pace. The country in these parts was flat, broken now and then by solitary shrubs, with here and there small stony hillocks. We rode without stopping until near midday, when suddenly my guide called out—

'Halt! Let the camels kneel down at once. Be quick!'

I stopped. The camels knelt.

'Why?'

194

'I see camels a long way off and two led horses, and fear we have been seen.'

I loaded my Remington to be prepared for any issue. 'But if we have been seen', I said, 'it is better to ride quietly on. Our making the animals lie down will excite their suspicion. In what direction are they going?'

'You are right,' said Hamed Ibn Hussein [another guide]. 'They are marching northwest.'

We rose and changed our line of march to the north-east, and were almost confident that we had passed unobserved when, to our despair, we perceived one of the party, which was about two thousand metres away from us, jump on his horse and gallop swiftly towards us.

'Hamed,' said I, 'I will go slowly on with Zeki. Do you stop the man, and answer his questions, and in any case prevent him from seeing me close. You have the money on you?'

'Good; but march slowly!'

I rode on quietly with Zeki, hiding my face with my *farda*, so as not to be recognised as a white man.

'Hamed is greeting the man, and has made his camel kneel,' said Zeki, looking back. After about twenty minutes, we saw the man remount his horse, and Hamed urging his camel on to rejoin us.

'You must thank God for our safety,' he cried, as he came up. 'The

195

man is a friend of mine, Mukhal, a Sheikh, on his way to Dongola with camels to bring dates to Omdurman. He asked me where I was going with the "white Egyptian". The man has the eyes of a hawk.'

'And what did you answer?'

'I adjured him as my friend to keep our secret, and gave him twenty Maria Theresa dollars. We Arabs are all a little avaricious. The man swore a sacred oath to me to hold his tongue if he happened to fall in with our pursuers; and his people are too far off to tell black from white. Urge the camels on; we have lost time.'

Lord Edward Cecil was called by his mother, Lady Salisbury, 'the stupidest and cleanest of my sons'. Someone replied that by normal standards he was very clever and rather dirty. In 1896 the Commander-in-Chief of the Egyptian Army, General Kitchener, decided to mount an expedition against the Khalifa's dervishes, partly to avenge General Gordon and partly to prevent the French from establishing a foothold on the upper Nile. He took the precaution of having Lord Edward as an aide-de-camp to ensure the support of Lord Salisbury, since many powerful figures were against intervention in the Sudan. Lord Edward describes the formidable character of Kitchener as displayed in the early stages of the campaign that ended in victory at Omdurman in 1898. After he became Commander-in-Chief in India in 1902 there were many who would have painted him as unscrupulous, devious and lazy.

I cannot truthfully say that I liked him at that period. He was much more uncouth and uncivilised at that time than he was later. He was always inclined to bully his own entourage, as some men are rude to their wives. The points that struck me as a simple onlooker were his aloofness, for he seemed to confide much in no one, and his extraordinary grasp of detail. It was almost true to say there was no department of the Egyptian Army which he did not know as well as the departmental officials; and though as a force it was tiny, a small force has just as many, or nearly as many, departments as a large one.

In his person he was very neat and always scrupulously clean. He tolerated laxity on these points with difficulty. On the other hand, his office was a sea of papers lying on tables, chairs, window-sills, the floor. I have heard him ask an officer whom he had sent for not to stand on the supplies returns.

He would wander off at that curious stalking stride of his soon after dawn to the railway yard, the embarkation place, the store yards, or whatever interested him for the minute. He saw everything—nothing escaped him; but he officially saw or did not see as much as he chose.

196

Kitchener as Sirdar (Commander) of the Egyptian Army in 1890, by von Herkomer

Sometimes he seemed to like one with him, but more often he liked to walk ahead, plunged apparently in sombre meditation. He usually got three good hours' work done before breakfast. He worked on then, except for lunch, till six in the evening, when he liked very often to have a gin or vermouth and soda and talk. It was his most human time. He would then go back to work till dinner, which might be at any hour, and went early to his room. Whether he worked habitually at night I don't know, but I often saw his light burning late.

In mind, from long experience of the East, he was cynical, and inclined to disbelieve that any action sprang from motives other than those of self-interest—or rather, he affected to be. He had in reality the greatest confidence in those who were worthy of it, and he was rarely if ever taken in. His cynicism was in a large measure a part of the curious shyness which declined to show any inside portion of his life or mind. He loathed any form of moral or mental undressing. He was even morbidly afraid of showing any feeling or enthusiasm, and he preferred to be misunderstood rather than be suspected of human feeling. Combined with this cynicism and suspicion, partly the result of many years' Eastern experience, and partly assumed as a cloak for other feelings, was a natural and almost childlike simplicity, both in his outlook on life and his display of what most of us hide with care.

We stayed first at Halfa for some time, and then gradually, as the river [Nile] rose and it was possible to bring up our boats, advanced, till finally we pushed back the dervishes and reached Dongola. It must not be imagined that the sailing was plain. The difficulty of supplying a force of even fifteen thousand men was immense; the only means of communication beyond camels (which then, as ever, died as fast as one could replace them, a camel being as fitted for regular supply transport work as a Bohemian for a domestic life) was a hastily laid railway, passing over very difficult country, with appalling gradients and curves, the rolling stock of which largely dated from the time of the Khedive Ismail. Thirty miles of this line were washed away in a night when we had only five days' rations for the whole army. Several of our best boats were much damaged coming through the cataracts, and the north wind was unusually late in starting that year, which made our sailing boats far slower than had been hoped. Cholera broke out, and at one time looked as if it would paralyse the whole operation. All through these disasters Kitchener's energy and determination never wavered, though he was querulous about them, with that queer simplicity to which I have alluded. He grumbled that he was doing his best, and if the powers above stopped him it was unfair and hard, and so on.

In December 1895 a foolhardy freelance attempt was made to topple the Boer regime in the Transvaal. The Boers easily defeated the 'Jameson Raid', as it was called, and kept control of the Rand goldmines around Johannesburg. The Kaiser sent a congratulatory telegram to Kruger, the Boer leader, but could do no more because of British naval supremacy. This strengthened his determination to build up the German Fleet. The raid had been instigated by Cecil Rhodes and his British South Africa Company, which had been busy colonising the area to the north of the Transvaal, including Matabeleland, taken from Chief Lobengula in 1893. The search for gold there was not successful, but this did not weaken British determination to keep possession when the Matabele rose in revolt in 1896. Among the officers taking part against the Matabele was Lieutenant-Colonel Robert Baden-Powell. He had first come to prominence the year before on a bloodless expedition in West Africa against King Prempeh of Kumasi. (One of Queen Victoria's favourite sons-in-law, Prince Henry of Battenberg, married to Princess Beatrice, died of malaria contracted on the march to Kumasi.) B.-P. first describes a typical encounter with the Matabele:

As we got nearer to the swarm of black heads among the grass and bushes, their rifles began to pop and their bullets to flit past with a weird little 'phit', 'phit', or a jet of dust and a shrill 'wh-e-e-e-w' where they ricocheted off the ground.

Some of our men, accustomed to mounted infantry work, were now for jumping off to return the fire, but the order was given: 'No; make a cavalry fight of it. Forward! Gallop!'

Then, as we came up close, the niggers let us have an irregular, rackety volley, and in another moment we were among them. They did not wait, but one and all they turned to fly, dodging in among the bushes, loading as they ran. And we were close upon their heels, zigzagging through the thorns, jumping off now and then, or pulling up, to fire a shot (we had not a sword among us, worse luck!), and on again.

Of course, besides their guns they had their assegais. Several of our horses got some wounds, and one man got a horrid stab straight into his stomach. I saw another of our men fling himself on to a Kaffir who was stabbing at him; together they rolled on the ground, and in a twinkling the white man had twisted the spear from its owner's hand, and after a short, sharp tussle, he drove it through the other's heart.

In one place one of the men got somewhat detached from the rest, and came on a bunch of eight of the enemy. These fired on him and killed his horse, but he himself was up in a trice, and, using magazine fire, he let them have it with such effect that before they could close on him with their clubs and assegais, he had floored half their number, and the rest just turned and fled.

I had my Colt's repeater with me—with only six cartridges in the magazine, and soon I found I had finished these—so, throwing it under a peculiar tree, where I might find it again, I went on with my revolver. Presently I came on an open stretch of ground, and about eighty yards before me was a Kaffir with a Martini-Henry. He saw me, and dropped on one knee and drew a steady bead on me. I felt so indignant at this that I rode at him as hard as I could go, calling him every name under the sun; he aimed—for an hour, it seemed to me—and it was quite a relief when at last he fired, at about ten yards' distance, and still more of a relief when I realised he had clean missed me. Then he jumped up and turned to run, but he had not gone two paces when he cringed as if someone had slapped him hard on the back, then his head dropped and his heels flew up, and he fell smack on his face, shot by one of our men behind me.

At last I called a halt. Our horses were done, the niggers were all scattered, and there were almost as many left behind us hiding in bushes as there were running on in front.

A few minutes spent in breathing the horses, and a vast amount of jabber and chaff, and then we reformed the line and returned at a walk, clearing the bush as we went.

Here, Baden-Powell gives some hints on the art of scouting, and what it can achieve:

Do not wear any bright colours about you. I noticed that after I had been on the sick list and resumed my scouting expeditions, the enemy caught sight of me much more quickly than they used to, though I took just as much care, and remained just as motionless; and I then came to the conclusion that this was due to the fact that I had, in accordance with the doctor's advice, taken to wearing a flannel cummerbund wound round my waist—and the only flannel at that time procurable was of a brilliant red; and this was what caught their eye.

Of course, anything liable to glitter or shine is fatal to concealment; rifle, pistol, field-glasses, wrist-watch, buckles, and buttons should be dulled, abolished, or held in such a way as not to catch the rays of the sun by day or of the moon by night.

For efficient scouting in rocky ground, in the dry season, india-rubber-soled shoes are essential; with these you can move in absolute silence, and over rocks which, from their smoothness or inclination, would be impassable with boots.

There is naturally a strong attraction in reconnoitring, for, apart from the fun of besting the enemy, the art of scouting is in itself as interesting as any detective work. A small instance will show my meaning as to what information can be read from trifling signs.

The other day, when out with my native scout, we came on a few downtrodden blades of common grass; this led us on to footprints in a sandy patch of ground. They were those of women or boys (judging from the size) on a long journey (they wore sandals), going towards the Matopos [hills]. Suddenly my boy gave a 'How!' of surprise, and ten yards off the track he picked up a leaf—it was the leaf of a tree that did not grow about here, but some ten or fifteen miles away; it was damp, and smelt of Kaffir beer. From these signs it was evident that women had been carrying beer from the place where the trees grew towards the Matopos (they stuff up the mouth of the beer-pots with leaves), and they had passed this way at four in the morning (a strong breeze had been blowing about that hour, and the leaf had evidently been blown ten yards away). This would bring them to the Matopos about five o'clock. The men would not delay to drink up the fresh beer, and would by this time be very comfortable, not to say half-stupid, and the reverse of on the *qui vive*; so that we were able to go and reconnoitre more nearly with impunity—all on the strength of information given by bruised grass and a leaf.

In 1897 there was a nasty little incident near the West African coast, not far from Lagos, when a British official on his way to sign a treaty with the King of Benin was ambushed and killed, along with a number of his entourage. The Royal Navy mounted a punitive expedition, and met with quite stiff resistance. As it approached Benin City it became apparent that the rest of the vice-consul's African porters who had been taken prisoner after the ambush were being ritually executed in a vain attempt to stop the advance of the blue jackets and marines. Benin was captured and, as well as copious evidence of human sacrifice, some two thousand pieces of sculpture were also found. These are the famous Benin bronzes, the most sophisticated art of sub-Saharan Africa. In the early years of the new century these bronzes, carried back to Europe as booty, together with ethnic art from other parts of the world, were to have a huge impact on the development of western art. The particular trophy selected to be given to Queen Victoria was not a bronze but a magnificent pair of ivory leopards, their spots made out of copper discs, that had once flanked the throne of the King of Benin.

One of Aubrey Beardsley's illustrations for Pope's poem The Rape of the Lock

Literature, Poetry
and Painting

E. F. Benson declared, talking of literature, that 'It was in this epoch for which "the Nineties" are a convenient expression that the long-retarded spring burst into fullest summer, and never has there been a more diverse flowering.' He then catalogued those who were active: Hardy, Wells, Meredith, Conrad, Barrie, Moore, Shaw, Wilde, Stevenson, James. The last three took a dim view of some of the newcomers, who drew upon the Empire for their inspiration and sought to take the revival of adventure fiction far beyond Treasure Island. *Henry James wrote to Robert Louis Stevenson in 1887 after reading Rider Haggard's* King Solomon's Mines *and* She, *set in the fierce landscape and among the fiercer tribes of southern Africa:*

Since I saw you I have finished *Solomon* and read half of *She*. Ah, *par exemple, c'est trop fort*—and the fortieth thousand on the title page of my *She* moves me to a holy indignation. It isn't nice that anything so vulgarly brutal should be the thing that succeeds most with the English of today. More even than with the contemptible inexpressiveness of the whole thing I am struck with the beastly *bloodiness* of it—or it comes back to the same thing—the cheapness of the hecatombs with which the genial narrative is bestrewn. Such perpetual killing and such perpetual ugliness! It is worthwhile to write a tale of fantastic adventure, with a funny man etc., and pitched all in the slangiest key, to kill twenty thousand men, as in *Solomon*, in order to help your heroes on! In *She* the Narrator himself shoots through the back (I think) his faithful servant Muhammad, to prevent his being boiled alive, and describes how he 'leaped into the air like a buck', on receiving the shot. He himself is addressed constantly by one of the personages of the tale as 'my Baboon'! *Quel genre!* They seem to me works in which our race and our age make a very vile figure.

*Robert Louis Ste-
venson painted by
Sargent in 1887,
just before he left for
America and the
South Seas*

When Rudyard Kipling's Plain Tales From the Hills *were published in
England in 1888, his uncle, Edward Burne-Jones, sent him a letter of congratulations: 'I read every line with deep interest and an admiration I
wouldn't qualify, even if I thought it good for your soul, so abundant it is
. . . Nothing is so nice as a book of little tales, when if they are tragical they
are not long enough to harrow the heart too much, and if they are merry,
the gods are not likely to envy us ten minutes' fun.' Writing in 1890, Oscar
Wilde was not so forbearing.*

As one turns over the pages of his *Plain Tales from the Hills*, one feels as
if one were seated under a palm tree reading life by superb flashes of vulgarity. The bright colours of the bazaars dazzle one's eyes. The jaded,
commonplace Anglo-Indians are in exquisite incongruity with their surroundings. The mere lack of style in the storyteller gives an odd journal-
istic realism to what he tells us. From the point of view of literature Mr
Kipling is a man of talent who drops his aspirates. From the point of view
of life he is a reporter who knows vulgarity better than anyone has ever
known it.

204

J. K. Stephen, Virginia Woolf's cousin, was equally unfair, longing for the moment

> When there stands a muzzled stripling
> Mute, beside a muzzled bore;
> When the Rudyards cease from Kipling
> And the Haggards ride no more.

Arthur Conan Doyle did not look so far afield when he wanted some sort of model for his detective. Instead of to Africa or India he turned to his days as a medical student in Edinburgh.

I thought of my old teacher Joe Bell, of his eagle face, of his curious ways, of his eerie trick of spotting details. If he were a detective he would surely reduce this fascinating but unorganised business to something nearer to an exact science. I would try if I could get this effect. It was surely possible in real life, so why should I not make it plausible in fiction? It is all very well to say that a man is clever, but the reader wants to see examples of it—such examples as Bell gave us every day in the wards. The idea amused me. What should I call the fellow? I still possess the leaf of a notebook with various alternative names. One rebelled against the elementary art which gives some inkling of character in the name, and creates Mr Sharps or Mr Ferrets. First it was Sherringford Holmes; then it was Sherlock Holmes. He could not tell his own exploits, so he must have a commonplace comrade as a foil—an educated man of action who could both join in the exploits and narrate them. A drab, quiet name for this unostentatious man. Watson would do. And so I had my puppets and wrote my *Study in Scarlet.*

Conan Doyle explains how Holmes was adapted from book to magazine publication, and goes on:

A number of monthly magazines were coming out at that time, notable among which was the *Strand.* Considering these various journals with their disconnected stories it had struck me that a single character running through a series, if it only engaged the attention of the reader, would bind that reader to that particular magazine. On the other hand, it had long seemed to me that the ordinary serial might be an impediment rather than a help to a magazine, since, sooner or later, one missed one number and afterwards it had lost all interest. Clearly the ideal compromise was a character which carried through, and yet instalments which were each complete in themselves, so that the purchaser was always sure

'I determined to end the life of my hero.' The scene in which Conan Doyle hoped he had disposed of Sherlock Holmes by sending him to his death at the Reichenbach Falls in Switzerland

that he could relish the whole contents of the magazine. I believe that I was the first to realise this and the *Strand* the first to put it into practice.

The difficulty of the Holmes work was that every story really needed as clear-cut and original a plot as a longish book would do. One cannot without effort spin plots at such a rate. At last, after I had done two series of them I saw that I was in danger of having my hand forced, and of being entirely identified with what I regarded as a lower stratum of literary achievement. Therefore as a sign of my resolution I determined to end the life of my hero. The idea was in my mind when I went with my wife for a short holiday in Switzerland, in the course of which we saw there the wonderful falls of Reichenbach, a terrible place, and one that I thought would make a worthy tomb for poor Sherlock, even if I buried my banking account along with him. So there I laid him, fully determined that he should stay there—as indeed for some years he did. I was amazed at the concern expressed by the public. They say that a man is never properly appreciated until he is dead, and the general protest against my summary execution of Holmes taught me how many and how

Alfred Tennyson in 1890

numerous were his friends. 'You Brute' was the beginning of the letter of remonstrance which one lady sent me, and I expect she spoke for others besides herself. I heard of many who wept.

People have often asked me whether I knew the end of a Holmes story before I started it. Of course I did. One could not possibly steer a course if one did not know one's destination. The first thing is to get your idea. Having got that key idea one's next task is to conceal it and lay emphasis upon everything which can make for a different explanation. Holmes, however, can see all the fallacies of the alternatives, and arrives more or less dramatically at the true solution by steps which he can describe and justify. He shows his powers by what the South Americans now call 'Sherlockholmitos', which means clever little deductions, which often have nothing to do with the matter in hand, but impress the reader with a general sense of power. The same effect is gained by his offhand allusion to other cases.

In the poetical world, both Robert Browning and Lord Tennyson were still

The Lady of Shalott, by J. W. Waterhouse. As late as 1888, when this was painted, Tennyson's verse was still a powerful inspiration to other artists

looming presences in 1887. Their 'party manners' make for a nice contrast. Tennyson was notoriously brusque: when the Cambridge don Oscar Browning introduced himself simply as 'Browning', Tennyson answered, 'No, you're not.' E. F. Benson tells of another occasion when

there was a young lady of the neighbourhood, the dream of whose romantic soul was to be introduced to him. Her heart's desire was granted her, and they sat down side by side on a garden seat. Dead silence fell: she was far too rapt and reverent and overpowered to speak, and he had nothing to say. Suddenly he found something to say, and he pronounced these appalling words, 'Your stays creak.'

Nearly swooning with horror and deeply hurt at this absolutely unfounded accusation, she fled from him without a word, and recovered her composure as best she might by converse with less alarming folk. Presently she observed that he was stalking her; she tripped from one gay group to another, and always the poet followed her, like a bloodhound on her trail. The dream of her soul had turned into a nightmare: certainly he was after her, and who could tell what he would say next?

Robert Browning

She dodged and she doubled, she hid behind trees, but she could not shake him off. Then she made a dreadful tactical error, for she scurried up a long path in the kitchen-garden hoping to distance him beyond pursuit, only to find that she had entered a cul-de-sac bordered by cabbages and asparagus and closed at the far end by the potting-shed. She fumbled at the latch, intending to hide herself from the dreadful presence, but it was locked, and now he closed in on her. 'I beg your pardon,' he said, 'it was my braces.'

Browning's urbanity, on the other hand, was hard to shake, even under great provocation, such as on the evening when, according to Augustus Hare, 'going down to dinner, the lady who fell to his share suddenly said to him, "You are a poet, aren't you?"—"Well, people are sometimes kind enough to say that I am."—"Oh, don't mind my having mentioned it: you know Lord Byron was a poet"'. G. W. E. Russell remembered when

Mr Browning had honoured me with his company at dinner, and an unduly fervent admirer had button-holed him throughout a long evening, plying him with questions about what he meant by this line, and whom he intended by that character. It was more than flesh and blood could stand, and at last the master extricated himself from the grasp of the disciple, exclaiming with the most airy grace, 'But, my dear fellow, this is too bad. *I* am monopolising *you*.'

Just before he died, however, Browning gave a final glimpse of the fire within. E. F. Benson again:

There had been published a [posthumous] volume of letters by the translator of Omar Khayyám, Edward FitzGerald; in it was one in which he wrote, 'Thank God Mrs Browning is dead; we shall have no more Aurora Leighs [one of her poems].' It was a bitter cross-grained way to put it, but all FitzGerald really meant was that he did not like Mrs Browning's poetry. He knew nothing of her, for they had never met, and there was no personal attack on her. But it was a crime to publish it during Browning's lifetime, for though the chance of his seeing it was small, the chance existed. He did see it, and published in the *Athenaeum* the following lines:

> I chanced upon a new book yesterday . . .
>   and learnt thereby
>   That you, FitzGerald, whom by ear and eye
> She never knew, thanked God my wife was dead.
>
> Aye, dead! and were yourself alive, good Fitz,
> How to return you thanks would pass my wits.
> Kicking you seems the common lot of curs,
>   While more appropriate greeting lends you grace.
>   Surely to spit there glorifies your face,
> Spitting with lips once sanctified by hers.

It is impossible not to feel a certain savage satisfaction. There was the old man nearer eighty than seventy; close on thirty years had passed since the death of his wife, but to him it was as if they had been but a watch in the night.

When Browning was buried in Poets' Corner in Westminster Abbey at the end of 1889, Burne-Jones deplored the ceremony, but recompense was made by the sequence of sonnets that Swinburne wrote on Browning's death.

No candles, no incense, no copes, no nothing that was nice. My dear, now they have got these churches they don't know what to do with them—placards all about saying 'Seats for the Press', 'Mourners'—all about. And the procession so poor and sorry! a canon four feet high next one of nine feet high—surplice, red hood like trousers down the back—you know them all. I would have given something for a banner or two, and much I would have given if a chorister had come out of the triforium and rent the air with a trumpet.

> Among the wondrous ways of men and time
>   He went as one that ever found and sought
>   And bore in hand the lamplike spirit of thought
> To illume with instance of its fire sublime
> The dusk of many a cloudlike age and clime.
>   No spirit in shape of light and darkness wrought,
>   No faith, no fear, no dream, no rapture, nought
> That blooms in wisdom, nought that burns in crime,
> No virtue girt and armed and helmed with light,
> No love more lovely than the snows are white,
>   No serpent sleeping in some dead soul's tomb,
> No song-bird singing from some live soul's height,
>   But he might hear, interpret, or illume
>   With sense invasive as the dawn of doom.

In 1892 Tennyson was laid beside Browning in Poets' Corner. In the last months before his death, a young army officer named Arthur Lee, later the Lord Lee who gave Chequers to be a country residence for British prime ministers, struck up a friendship with the old poet.

I told him I had often been full of doubts and how 'In Memoriam' had helped me; at which he said suddenly and vehemently: 'I too am always full of doubts; I know not what to believe' . . . [Tennyson said that in his youth socialism was even more rampant than now, adding] 'When I was a little boy I heard our country coachman say that he would like to go up to London to be there when they cut the throats of the quality.' One day he stopped under a large laburnum tree in full bloom and said almost querulously, pointing at the blossoms, 'Why should I not describe these as "dropping wells of fire"? The man accused me of inaccurate imagery. Has he no ideas beyond the coal fire in his own grate at home?' Stopping one day under some telegraph wires through which the high wind was humming, he said: 'Listen to the spirits wailing in the wires, carrying their message of grief and woe far and wide and darkening homes with the sorrows which they bear.'

Tennyson's death meant that the post of Poet Laureate, which he had held since taking it over from Wordsworth in 1850, fell vacant. Swinburne was the obvious choice, but had ruled himself out because of his earlier excesses and paganism, as had William Morris, on the grounds of his socialism. On Arthur Balfour's recommendation, Lord Salisbury offered the Laureateship to Kipling after it had remained vacant for some years, but he turned it down and the post went instead to a conceited buffoon named Alfred Austin. Robert Browning told a story of how once, a butler having announced the diminutive Austin at a grand gathering, 'I give you my word of honour, nothing whatever *came into the room.' E. F. Benson was equally dismissive of him:*

When Lord Salisbury was asked for what sort of reason he had appointed Mr Alfred Austin, he is reported to have said (with thoughtful candour), 'I don't think anybody else applied for the post.' His opinion both of the candidate and of the office to which he had presented him could thereby be accurately gauged. My family were deeply interested in this appointment, for a short time before it was announced the poet had stayed with us. I am afraid we formed the design of drawing out Mr Austin when he came to the smoking-room that night and getting all we could out of him. But there was no need to put this treacherous scheme into practice, for Mr Austin poured himself out, of his own spontaneous uncorking, with a fullness and a foam that our clumsy handling could never have accomplished. He laid himself down, all five feet of him on the sofa, and as feast-master directed a wondrous symposium entirely about himself.

Mr Austin began to tell us of 'It'. 'It' was the poetic inspiration. Sometimes It left him altogether, and when that first happened he was terribly upset, for he feared that he would be able to write no more poetry, since he never wrote a line except when It directed him. But he had learned since then that, though It might leave him for a while, It always returned, and so he waited without fretting or attempting to produce uninspired stuff, until It came back. The Jameson Raid inspired a fugitive composition, and It was surely there when Mr Austin wrote:

> They went across the veldt,
> As hard as they could pelt.

To him, too, is ascribed, though with what certainty I know not, a wonderful couplet concerning the national suspense during the illness of the Prince of Wales in 1871: the internal evidence strongly supports the theory.

Across the wires the electric message came,
He is no better, he is much the same.

That sounds very like It: that sounds like Mr Austin at his very best.

Austin was appointed Laureate in 1896, but that year was saved from going down in poetic annals as one of infamy by the publication of A Shropshire Lad *by A. E. Housman. Showing the utmost brilliance in the classical part of his degree at Oxford, Housman was unable to take the philosophical part seriously, and instead of being snapped up immediately for an academic post, he had to spend long years drudging in the Patents Office before becoming Professor of Latin at University College, London in 1892. There were several strands to his inspiration: he had an unassuageable yearning for the past, and for some imagined Shropshire landscape of hills and woods — he wrote quite a number of the poems in the book before he had even visited the county. The death of his father in 1894 obviously acted as a release mechanism and, as a homosexual, he was also stimulated by the trial of Oscar Wilde in 1895. This last strand had to be left implicit in his melancholy verses on lads, lasses, and young soldiers — he had a brother serving in the ranks. But those on the lookout saw it clearly enough: a friend of Oscar Wilde learnt some of the poems by heart and recited them to him in Reading Gaol.*

Loveliest of trees, the cherry now
Is hung with bloom along the bough,
And stands about the woodland ride
Wearing white for Eastertide.

In summertime on Bredon
The bells they sound so clear;
Round both the shires they ring them
In steeples far and near,
A happy noise to hear.

On Wenlock Edge the wood's in trouble;
His forest fleece the Wrekin heaves;
The gale, it plies the saplings double,
And thick on Severn snow the leaves.

Much is made of the 1890s as the decade of the decadents, poets determined to push to the limits the earlier Aesthetic movement's ideas of Art for Art's sake, adopting the French Symbolist justification of excess if it led to beauty. But little enough has stood the test of time from the work inspired by the absinthe of the Café Royal or the pint tankards of the Cheshire Cheese, two favourite haunts. Exceptions can be made for Richard Le Gallienne's 'Beauty Accursed':

> I am so fair that whereso'er I wend
> Men yearn with strange desire to kiss my face,
> Stretch out their hands to touch me as I pass,
> And women follow me from place to place.
>
> The sleepy kine move round me in desire
> And press their oozy lips upon my hair,
> Toads kiss my feet, and creatures of the mire,
> The snails will leave their shells to watch me there.

And for Ernest Dowson's 'Cynara':

> I have forgot much, Cynara! gone with the wind,
> Flung roses, roses, riotously, with the throng,
> Dancing to put thy pale lost lilies out of mind;
> But I was desolate and sick of an old passion,
> Yea, all the time because the dance was long,
> I have been faithful to thee, Cynara! in my fashion.

Francis Thompson was a special case because, although addicted to laudanum, he was also possessed by Roman Catholicism, which does not consort happily with ideas of decadence. The landscapes in his 'Hound of Heaven' must echo the Piranesian architecture of his opiate dreams.

> I fled Him, down the nights and down the days;
> I fled Him, down the arches of the years;
> I fled Him, down the labyrinthine ways
> Of my own mind; and in the mist of tears
> I hid from Him, and under running laughter.
>   Up vistaed hopes I sped;
>   And shot, precipitated,
> Adown titanic glooms of chasmed fears,
>   From those strong Feet that followed, followed after.

The periodical that, above all others, is connected with the Nineties is The Yellow Book, *but to see it as the house magazine of the decadents, bent on artistic upheaval, is very wide of the mark. As E. F. Benson said, it was*

One of Beardsley's cover designs for The Savoy *magazine*

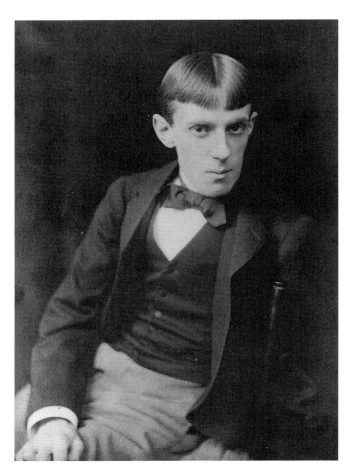

'an interesting illustrated quarterly the first number of which appeared in April 1894, [and] so far from being a revolutionary gazette [it] was a respectable, almost high-brow organ, and its contributors for the most part no more rebels against Victorian conventions than the Queen herself.' The one exception to this was Aubrey Beardsley, whose work illustrated the magazine. If any one figure from the Nineties really earned the decadent label, it was he by his brilliant, unmistakable drawings, combining strength and delicacy of line with refined yet blatant sexuality. Beardsley emerged in London at the start of the decade after a youth of genteel impoverishment on the South Coast, already in the grip of the tuberculosis that was to kill him a few years later. William Rothenstein, an artist who also made his name at this time, recalled him:

Beardsley, now that we look back on his few years of hectic, hurried life, is a touching and lovable figure. But at the time, with his butterfly ties, his too smart clothes with their hard, padded shoulders, his face—as Oscar said—'like a silver hatchet' under his spreading chestnut hair, parted in the middle and arranged low over his forehead, his staccato voice and jumpy, restless manners, he appeared a portent of change—symbolic of

216

the movement which was associated—and was to end—with the last years of the century.

In July 1891 Beardsley described his big break into the artistic world:

Yesterday I and my sister went to see the studio of Burne-Jones, as I had heard that admittance might be gained to see the pictures by sending in one's visiting card. When we arrived however we were told that the studio had not been open for some years and that we could not see Mr Burne-Jones without a special appointment. So we left somewhat disconsolately.

I had hardly turned the corner when I heard a quick step behind me, and a voice which said, 'Pray come back, I couldn't think of letting you go away without seeing the pictures, after a journey on a hot day like this.' The voice was that of Burne-Jones, who escorted us back to his house and took us into the studio, showing and explaining everything. His kindness was wonderful as we were perfect strangers, he not even knowing our names.

By the merest chance I happened to have some of my best drawings with me, and I asked him to look at them and give me his opinion. After he had examined them for a few minutes he exclaimed, 'There is *no* doubt about your gift, one day you will most assuredly paint very great and beautiful pictures. All are *full* of thought, poetry and imagination. Nature has given you every gift which is necessary to become a great artist. I *seldom* or *never* advise anyone to take up art as a profession, but in *your* case *I can do nothing else.*' And all this from the greatest living artist in Europe.

Afterwards we returned to the lawn and had afternoon tea. Mrs Burne-Jones is very charming. The Oscar Wildes and several others were there. All congratulated me on my success, as 'Mr Burne-Jones is a very severe critic.'

Soon Beardsley was commissioned to do illustrations for Wilde's Salomé, *but, according to William Rothenstein, Wilde 'thought them too Japanese, as indeed they were. His play was Byzantine.' His patrons could not keep up with the speed at which Beardsley was changing his style: 'The inspiration of Morris and Burne-Jones was waning fast, and the eighteenth-century illustrators were taking the place of the Japanese print.' In February 1893 Beardsley described his style as 'something suggestive of Japan, but not really japonesque . . . The subjects were quite mad and a little indecent. Strange hermaphroditic creatures wandering about in Pierrot costumes or modern dress; quite a new world of my own creation.'*

Love leading the
Pilgrim, *by Edward
Burne-Jones*

*At the end of that year Burne-Jones fell out with him, as he recalled in
1898 after Beardsley's death:*

I asked him how he was getting on with the book he was decorating—
King Arthur that was—and he said he'd be precious glad when it was
done, he hated it so. So I asked him, why did he do it, and he said
because he'd been asked. He hated the story and he hated all medieval
things—and I said, how could it be successful work then. I never saw
such a pitiful exhibition of vanity in my life. I wondered why it was he
took the trouble to come and see me, unless it was to show off and let me
know my influence with him was over. As if it mattered in the least
whether it was or not. Then he got into all that horrid set of semi-
sodomites, and after Oscar Wilde's disappearance had almost to disappear himself. Damned young fool. In one season he was suddenly
marched into that ridiculous position of his that was entirely invented by
critics, and he believed it all.

*As Burne-Jones implies by his remarks, the trial of Oscar Wilde caused the
publisher of* The Yellow Book *to take fright and drop Beardsley, the one
contributor who had really lent it distinction, after four issues. He now
came under the aegis of Leonard Smithers, a publisher who mixed porno-
graphy with works of genuine quality. Wilde called him 'the most learned
erotomaniac in Europe'. Smithers set up* The Savoy *magazine and in it
Beardsley's work continued to astonish, whether his brilliant cover
designs, or his illustrations for Pope's* Rape of the Lock. *He also did
eight erotic illustrations for Smithers's edition of Aristophanes' play the*
Lysistrata. *It was all too much for Burne-Jones who, after looking at some*

A cartoon by Edward Burne-Jones celebrating completion of the Kelmscott Chaucer. The poet bestows his benison on William Morris (left) and Burne-Jones

Beardsley drawings, declared, 'they were more lustful than any I've seen — not that I've seen many. There was a woman with breasts each larger than her head, which was quite tiny and features insignificant, so that she looked like a mere lustful animal. Lust does frighten me, I must say. It looks like such despair.' Some would say that therein lay the flaw in Burne-Jones's own art: that his figures were bloodless, wan and listless; that, in Augustus Hare's words, he was 'the painter of morbid and unlovely women, who had given an apotheosis to ennui — the Botticelli of the nine-teenth century'. Others are happy to accept his own definition of a picture as 'a beautiful romantic dream, something that never was, never will be, in a light better than any light that ever shone, in a land no one can define or remember — only desire'. Whether in the Briar Rose series, King Arthur in Avalon, or the Adventures of Perseus, they succumb to his haunting spell.

Perhaps Burne-Jones's greatest act of homage to his vision of the Middle Ages was The Kelmscott Chaucer. The designer and poet William Morris, who managed to be a fervent medievalist as well as socialist and to whom Burne-Jones had been devoted since their days at Oxford, established the Kelmscott Press in 1890. They had dreamt of making a beautiful book together since their student days and in 1891 embarked on the Chaucer. Burne-Jones said, 'my share in it is that of the carver of the images in Amiens, and Morris's that of the architect.' In 1895 he speculated:

Carnation, Lily, Lily,
Rose, *by Sargent*

I wonder, if Chaucer were alive now or is aware of what is going on, whether he'd be satisfied with my pictures to his book, or whether he'd prefer Impressionist ones. I don't trust him, and if he and Mr Morris were to meet in Heaven, I wonder if they'd quarrel. I hope Botticelli and I would get on together; Michael Angelo would sniff contemptuously at me, I know . . . I know not ten people in the land will care twopence about it [the *Chaucer*]. But I think about the year 2133, there will be a passing craze for it.

The book, including Burne-Jones's eighty-seven illustrations, was completed the following year, just before Morris died.

The American-born James Whistler's greatest period was really over by 1887, though he was still capable of wonderful things in oil, watercolour, etching or lithograph. His erstwhile disciple, Walter Sickert, was, like Max Beerbohm, deep in a love affair with the music hall at this time. In 1886 another expatriate American painter, the thirty-year-old John Singer Sargent, settled permanently in London after a portrait which he had exhibited at the Paris Salon met with disapproval. His art now went in two directions: he continued to paint dazzling portraits of the utmost accomplishment, and also embarked on an excursion into Impressionism, no doubt influenced by his friendship with Claude Monet. His marvellously decorative Carnation, Lily, Lily, Rose, *combining French Impressionist with English Aesthetic influences, triumphed at the Royal Academy in 1887, and he captured the current 'boating' craze, painting his friends on the Avon and the Thames. Henry James, who had taken Sargent under his wing when he visited London in 1884, by 1887 was obviously disturbed by some of these developments in his protégé and found himself*

wondering whether it is an advantage to an artist to obtain early in life such possession of his means that the struggle with them ceases to exist for him. May not this breed a wantonness, an irreverence—what is vulgarly termed a 'larkiness'—on the part of the youthful genius who has, as it were, all his fortune in his pocket? . . . He knows so much about the art of painting that he perhaps does not fear emergencies quite enough, and having knowledge to spare, he may be tempted to play with it and waste it. Various, curious, as we have called him, he occasionally tries experiments which seem to arise from the mere high spirits of his brush, and runs risks little courted by the votaries of the literal, who never expose their necks to escape from the common.

A souvenir advertisement put out by the patent medicine firm founded by Thomas Holloway. An archetypal Victorian figure, he founded a women's college and an insane asylum with his wealth

1897: The Diamond Jubilee

The second Jubilee was a much greater affair than that of 1887. Lytton Strachey suggested the reason why:

Victoria understood very well the meaning and the attractions of power and property, and in such learning the English nation, too, had grown to be more and more proficient. During the last fifteen years of the reign— for the short Liberal Administration of 1892 was a mere interlude— Imperialism was the dominant creed of the country. It was Victoria's as well. Imperialism is a faith as well as a business; as it grew, the mysticism in English public life grew with it; and simultaneously a new importance began to attach to the Crown. The need for a symbol—a symbol of England's might, of England's worth, of England's extraordinary and mysterious destiny—became felt more urgently than ever before. The Crown was that symbol: and the Crown rested upon the head of Victoria.

The little old lady, with her white hair and her plain mourning clothes, in her wheeled chair or her donkey-carriage—one saw her so . . . That was the familiar vision, and it was admirable; but, at chosen moments, it was right that the widow of Windsor should step forth apparent Queen. The last and the most glorious of such occasions was the Jubilee of 1897.

Indeed, at the banquet at Buckingham Palace on the eve of the Jubilee, on 21 June, the Queen did not wear black, for the first time in her widowhood. On 22 June, escorted by fifty thousand troops, she went north of the river to St Paul's where she remained in her carriage whilst a Te Deum *was sung, before returning over London Bridge and south of the Thames. The sun came out at St Paul's and the occasion was recorded on the new cinematograph. As might be expected, Lady Monkswell did not miss out on the procession.*

First came the Naval Brigade with guns, and the ten or twelve colonial premiers and their wives in carriages, each followed by the mounted

The Queen arriving at the steps of St Paul's Cathedral for the Diamond Jubilee service. On the way there had been cries from the crowd of 'Go it, old girl'. Painting by John Charlton

troops of their colony, such strange, fine looking horsemen. The excellent premiers and their wives who in their continent are quite small people, had never had such a good day in their lives, and were chiefly grinning from ear to ear with joy and pride. They were very well cheered. Secondly came Captain Ames, the tallest man in the British Army, six feet eight inches, and his four troopers, seven or eight batteries of Horse Artillery, divided by what seemed to my aching sight endless squadrons of Dragoon Guards, Hussars, the Scots Greys, and the 17th Lancers. Thirdly the splendid troops of native Indian Cavalry, the Indian princes in their magnificent native costumes and riding the most splendid horses. The last, riding alone, was Sir Pertab Singh, ADC to the Prince of Wales, and the great polo player. He looked one mass of gold—and the sixteen carriages ending with the cream coloured ponies, and the Queen. She was sitting quite upright and brisk in the carriage, not looking flushed or overcome, but smiling and bowing. She was dressed in grey and black, and held in her hand the very long-handled black lace parasol lined with white, given her by Mr Charles Villiers, the oldest MP. She held it high up so that we could see her face.

Edward Burne-Jones was also a spectator, but a more critical one than Lady Monkswell.

224

It was all surprisingly successful—but all the boasting of the papers is so dreadful; it makes one wonder that a thunderbolt doesn't fall upon London. They're so silly as not to know that the gods do not love the pride of cockiness. And all this enthusiasm spent over one little unimportant old lady in the one effort of imagination of the English race. It's curious, but rather pretty. There was one set of men near where we were, that won great favour. It was a regiment that kept the ground in front of Downing Street—the Seaforth Highlanders. They were in the highest good humour with everybody, and the pipers puffed away and kept walking backwards and forwards swelling with such pride and excitement that their naked calves seemed to turn upwards—making such a beastly row that I loathe and detest above all others—till I nearly went mad. Excellent people no doubt and in the best of tempers they were, but in that dress with tight plaid trousers and huge head-dress of ostrich feathers they looked like South Sea Islanders altogether. There was an old boy on horseback who kept riding up and down and screaming at them and you could see his ridiculous bottom as he sat on his saddle. And he had brass-coloured eyebrows and moustaches and a pink face.

Celebrations were not confined to London: on 23 June Oscar Wilde wrote to Alfred Douglas from Dieppe about the party he had given for local children the day before (Sebastian Melmoth was the name he had assumed).

My darling Boy, Thanks for your letter received this morning. My *fête* was a huge success: fifteen *gamins* were entertained on strawberries and cream, apricots, chocolates, cakes, and *sirop de grenadine*. I had a huge iced cake with *Jubilé de la Reine Victoria* in pink sugar just rosetted with green, and a great wreath of red roses round it all. Every child was asked beforehand to choose his present: they all chose instruments of music!!! *6 accordions, 5 trompettes, 4 clairons.* They sang the Marseillaise and other songs, and danced a *ronde*, and also played 'God save the Queen': they said it was 'God save the Queen', and I did not like to differ from them. They also all had flags which I gave them. They were most gay and sweet. I gave the health of *La Reine d'Angleterre*, and they cried '*Vive la Reine d'Angleterre*'!!!! Then I gave '*La France, mère de tous les artistes*', and finally I gave *Le Président de la République*: I thought I had better do so. They cried out with one accord '*Vivent le Président de la République et Monsieur Melmoth*'!!! So I found my name coupled with that of the President. It was an amusing experience as I am hardly more than a month out of gaol.

On 28 June there was a garden party at Buckingham Palace. Lady Monkswell once more:

Indian cavalry officers were there in great numbers, splendid men in handsome uniforms and long boots. The Queen got into a large victoria drawn by two greys; an outrider on a very quiet sensible knowing old grey went first. She went all round the garden, everybody crowding round and curtseying in a way which must have satisfied her inmost heart. She then went and sat in a large tent banked up with flowers; it was wide open—all the front—and her faithful subjects could see her taking her tea and having her toast buttered by the Indian servant.

Another large marquee there was not open, and became stifling. Reginald Brett, Lord Esher, was present in his Court dress, which included a rapier. He drew it and used it to cut openings in the canvas, until stopped by a yell from a royal housemaid on the far side whom he had inadvertently stabbed.

On 30 June the Colonial Secretary, Joseph Chamberlain, the dust not long settled from his involvement in the Jameson Raid, gave a party. The journalist Sir Henry Lucy recorded it in his diary the next day:

Mrs Chamberlain's party last night was 'to have the honour of meeting their Royal Highnesses the Prince and Princess of Wales' . . . The fact is that their Royal Highnesses, having made several attempts to approach the entrance of 103 Piccadilly, finally gave up the attempt and quietly, perhaps gratefully, went off home. Chamberlain, whose ideas in these later times are all on an Imperial scale, incurred vast expense in hiring [it but] it did not prove nearly large enough . . . The night was oppressively hot. [A] thunderstorm . . . still loured sullen and unbroken over London. The first impulse of guests on entering the rooms was to get out again. The Duchess of Devonshire, whose enterprise and perseverance nothing can withstand, made early escape by a back stairway . . . It led to the kitchen and grand dames hurrying down were brushed against by servants carrying up dinner. Some having reached the basement munched stray sandwiches, and even more gratefully accepted other refreshment from waiters bustling by with bottles and jugs.

The grandest party was the Duchess of Devonshire's own, a fancy dress ball on 2 July. This time the Prince and Princess of Wales were there, as was the aristocracy in depth, and the Souls. Herbert Asquith went, rather menacingly, as a Roundhead soldier, his wife Margot as an oriental snake charmer. The person who had least worry over his outfit was Henry Irving: he merely had to don his costume as Cardinal Wolsey.

The new Poet Laureate, Alfred Austin, wrote a predictably dreadful

226

poem on the Jubilee, but so did Francis Thompson. His began 'Night; and the street a corpse beneath the moon', and never really recovered:

> Come hither, proud and ancient East,
> Gather ye to this Lady of the North,
> And sit down with her at her solemn feast,
> Upon this culminant day of all her days;
> For ye have heard the thunder of her goings-forth,
> And wonder of her large imperial ways.

The Queen in the garden at Osborne with three future kings: her son, later George V, holds his son, Bertie, later George VI. His other son, the future Edward VIII, is third from left

The situation was redeemed by Kipling. He had begun 'Recessional' actually on 22 June, only to put it to one side while he went to sea with the Channel Fleet (pp.176–7). At some point he must have sent it to Rider Haggard, because on 10 July Kipling wrote to him:

My objection to that hymn is that it may be quoted as an excuse for lying down abjectly at all times and seasons and taking what any other country may think fit to give us. What I wanted to say was: 'Don't gas, but be ready to give people snuff '—and I only covered the first part of the notion.

227

On 16 July Kipling went so far as to throw the manuscript in the waste-paper basket, only for Sarah Norton, daughter of his friend Professor Charles Eliot Norton of Harvard, to retrieve it. Kipling was persuaded by her and Edward Burne-Jones's wife Georgiana to revise it somewhat and then send it to The Times, *where it was published the next day.*

> Far-called, our navies melt away;
> On dune and headland sinks the fire:
> Lo, all our pomp of yesterday
> Is one with Nineveh and Tyre!
> Judge of the nations, spare us yet,
> Lest we forget—lest we forget!

Kipling's ambivalence about 'Recessional' was repeated in two letters that he wrote on 21 July. The first was to Moberly Bell, the manager of The Times: *'I entirely and absolutely agree with your Berlin ex-correspondent. By all means let us kick the Germans — "lest we forget" . . . When I think of the pious hymn I am astounded at my own moderation.' The second letter was to Burne-Jones's son-in-law, J. W. Mackail, a radical with strong reservations about Britain's Imperialism, who had written saying he feared the country was heading for a 'big smash', blinded by all the flag-waving sentiment of the Jubilee, and congratulating Kipling for sounding a warning note. Kipling replied: 'The big smash is coming one of these days, sure enough, but I think we shall pull through not without credit. It will be the common people – the third-class carriages – that'll save us.' Whatever satisfaction Kipling got from the way his 'hymn' was received, it paled by comparison with his joy at the birth of a longed-for son, John, in August. Seventeen years later the 'big smash' came, the first-, second- and third-class carriages went to war against Germany, and Kipling lost his son, a subaltern in the Irish Guards.*

But this was far over the horizon. For the moment it seemed quite appropriate that while the Prince of Wales had ridden on one side of his mother's carriage on the drive to St Paul's, the Kaiser had ridden on the other. The London and North Western Railway erected decorations which spelt out 'Longest, Noblest, Wisest Reign', and the Queen's subjects heartily concurred, whether they spotted the subliminal message or not. A story first told by the Bishop of Winchester,* and soon circulating in the West End clubs, can only have enhanced its hearers' affection for their monarch: 'The Queen asked him "From what point did you see the procession?" then recollecting, she said, "Oh! you were on the steps of St Paul's. I", she added, "was unfortunate – I had a very bad place and saw nothing."'
*As reported by Sir Mountstuart Grant Duff.

Illustrations

229

230

232

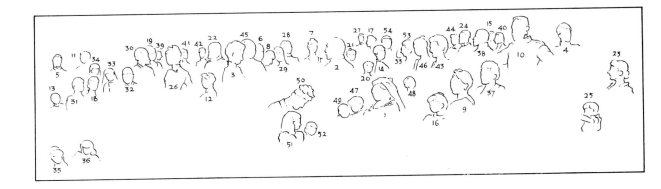

Key to page 106

234

Sources

Every effort has been made to contact copyright holders; in the event of an inadvertent omission or error, the editorial department should be notified at The Folio Society, 44 Eagle Street, London WC1R 4FS.

The editor wishes to thank the following writers, publishers and literary representatives for their permission to use copyright material:

Margot Asquith, *Autobiography*, 1920

Robert Baden-Powell, *The Matabele Campaign*, 1896

Arthur Balfour, *Chapters of Autobiography*, 1930

Aubrey Beardsley, *Letters*, 1970 (first published by Cassell)

Max Beerbohm, *A Peep into the Past*, 1972 (by permission of Mrs Eva Reichmann, see p. 172)

——*Around Theatres*, Vol II, 1924 (by permission of Mrs Eva Reichmann, see pp. 146–7)

——*Letters to Reggie Turner*, 1964 (by permission of Mrs Eva Reichmann, see pp. 166–7)

——*Mainly on the Air*, 1947 (by permission of Mrs Eva Reichmann, see pp. 141–5)

E. F. Benson, *As We Were*, 1930

Annie Besant, *Link*, June 23, 1888

Charles Booth, *Life and Labour of the People in London*, 1902

Reginald Brett, *see* Viscount Esher

Edward Burne-Jones and Thomas Rooke, *Burne-Jones Talking*, 1982 (by permission of John Murray (Publishers) Ltd, see pp. 218–9 and 224–5)

Georgiana Burne-Jones, *Memorials of Edward Burne-Jones*, 1904

Sydney Buxton, *Fishing and Shooting*, 1902

Mrs Patrick Campbell, *My Life and Some Letters*, 1925

Neville Cardus, *The Essential Neville Cardus*, 1949 (by permission of Sir Rupert Hart-Davis, see pp. 135–6)

Lord Edward Cecil, *The Leisure of an Egyptian Official*, 1921

Lady Gwendolen Cecil, *Life of Robert, Marquis of Salisbury*, 1921–32

Winston Churchill, *My Early Life*, 1941 (by permission of Curtis Brown on behalf of Winston S. Churchill. Copyright The Estate of Sir Winston S. Churchill, 1930. See pp. 145–6 and 187–92)

Richard Dorment, *Alfred Gilbert*, 1985

Arthur Conan Doyle, *Memories and Adventures*, 1924

Tiny Grant Duff, *see* Anne Freemantle

Timothy Eden, *The Tribulations of a Baronet*, 1933 (by permission of Lord Eden, see p. 139–40)

Viscount Esher, *Journals and Letters*, 1934

Anne Freemantle, *Three-Cornered Heart*, 1971

Alfred Gilbert, *see* Richard Dorment

Honor Godfrey, *Tower Bridge*, 1988

Lord Ronald Gower, *Old Diaries 1881–1901*, 1902

Philip Guedalla, *The Queen and Mr Gladstone*, 1933

Rolt Hammond, *The Forth Bridge*, 1964

Augustus Hare, *The Story of My Life*, 1900

Charles Hobhouse, *Inside Asquith's Cabinet*, 1977

Anthony Hope, *The Dolly Dialogues*, 1894

Henry James, *Letters Vol. III 1883–95*, 1981

Harper's New Monthly Magazine, October 1887

Jerome K. Jerome, *My Life and Times*, 1926

L. E. Jones, *A Victorian Boyhood*, 1955 (by permission of Macmillan General Books, see pp. 89–91)

Rudyard Kipling, *A Fleet in Being*, 1898 (by permission of A. P. Watt Ltd on behalf of The National Trust for Places of Historic Interest or Natural Beauty, see pp. 176–81)

——extract from *Recessional*, 1897 (by permission of A. P. Watt Ltd on behalf of The National Trust for Places of Historic Interest or Natural Beauty, see p. 228)

——*Letters*, Vol II, 1990 (by permission of A. P. Watt Ltd on behalf of The National Trust for Places of Historic Interest or Natural Beauty, see pp. 12 and 228)

——*Rudyard Kipling to Rider Haggard* (ed. Morton Cohen), 1965 (by permission of A. P. Watt Ltd on behalf of The National Trust for Places of Historic Interest or Natural Beauty, see p. 227)

Angela Lambert, *Unquiet Souls*, 1984

Viscount Lee of Fareham, *A Good Innings*, 1974 (by permission of John Murray (Publishers) Ltd, see pp. 52–3, 125–6, 223–4 and 225–6)

Henry Lucy, *Diary of a Journalist*, 1920

Emily Lutyens (Lytton), *A Blessed Girl*, 1953 (by permission of Mrs J. G. Links, see pp. 37–9, 123–4, 135 and 152)

Edith, Countess of Lytton, *Lady Lytton's Court Diary*, 1961 (by permission of Mrs J. G. Links, see p. 94)

Marie Mallet, *Life With Queen Victoria*, 1968 (by permission of John Murray (Publishers) Ltd, see pp. 94–7, 99–100 and 113–4)

Mary, Lady Monkswell, *A Victorian Diarist 1873–95*, 1944

——*A Victorian Diarist 1895–1909*, 1946 (by permission of John Murray (Publishers) Ltd, see pp. 52–3, 125–6, 223–4 and 225–6)

Arthur Morrison, *A Child of the Jago*, 1896

Arthur Ponsonby, *Henry Ponsonby*, 1942

Beatrix Potter, *Journal*, 1966 (by permission of the publishers Frederick Warne & Co., see pp. 15–16)

Beatrice Potter, *see* Charles Booth

Agatha Ramm (ed.), *Beloved and Darling Child*, the correspondence between Queen Victoria and her daughter, the Empress Frederick of Germany, 1886–1901, 1990

Michaela Reid, *Ask Sir James*, a biography of Sir James Reid, 1987

W. Graham Robertson, *Time Was*, 1931 (by permission of Penguin Books Ltd, see pp. 151–3, 155, 158–65)

William Rothenstein, *Men and Memories*, 1931

G. W. E. Russell, *Collections and Recollections*, 1898

Rudolf von Slatin, *Fire and Sword in the Sudan*, 1896

Lytton Strachey, *Queen Victoria*, 1921

Helena Swanwick, *I Have Been Young*, 1935

Christopher Sykes, *Four Studies in Loyalty*, 1946

Ellen Terry, *Memoirs*, 1933

Frances, Countess of Warwick, *Life's Ebb and Flow*, 1929

——*Afterthoughts*, 1931

Oscar Wilde, *Letters*, 1962 (by permission of Merlin Holland. © The Estate of Oscar Wilde 1962. See pp. 170–1 and 225)

Lady Wilson, *Letters From India*, 1911

Lord and Lady Wolseley, *Letters*, 1923

Index